WITHDRAWN

FRIENDS

SCRAPBOOKING TECHNIQUES

Sewing on Paper

C & J

FAITH ❋ HOPE ❋ LOVE

love is patient

love is kind and envies no one.
Love is never boastful, nor conceited,
nor rude; never selfish,
not quick to take offense.
There is nothing love cannot face;
there is no limit to its faith,
its hope, and endurance.
In a word, there are three things
that last forever: faith, hope, and love;
but the greatest of them all is love.

~ 1 Corinthians 13 ~

SCRAPBOOKING TECHNIQUES

Sewing on paper

Catherine Matthews-Scanlon

A LARK/CHAPELLE BOOK

A Division of Sterling Publishing Co., Inc.
New York

A Lark/Chapelle Book

Chapelle, Ltd., Inc.
P.O. Box 9255, Ogden, UT 84409
(801) 621-2777 • (801) 621-2788 Fax
e-mail: chapelle@chapelleltd.com
Web site: www.chapelleltd.com

Library of Congress Cataloging-in-Publication Data

Matthews-Scanlon, Catherine.
Scrapbooking techniques : sewing on paper / Catherine Matthews-
Scanlon. --
1st ed.
    p. cm.
Includes index.
ISBN 1-57990-987-6 (hardcover)
1. Photograph albums. 2. Scrapbooks. 3. Sewing. I. Title.
TR501.M38 2006
745.593--dc22

                                        2006015069

10 9 8 7 6 5 4 3 2 1

First Edition

Published by Lark Books, A Division of
Sterling Publishing Co., Inc.
387 Park Avenue South, New York, N.Y. 10016

©2006 by Catherine Matthews-Scanlon

Distributed in Canada by Sterling Publishing,
c/o Canadian Manda Group, 165 Dufferin Street
Toronto, Ontario, Canada M6K 3H6

Distributed in the United Kingdom by GMC Distribution Services,
Castle Place, 166 High Street, Lewes, East Sussex, England BN7 1XU

Distributed in Australia by Capricorn Link (Australia) Pty Ltd.,
P.O. Box 704, Windsor, NSW 2756 Australia

Manufactured in China

ISBN 13: 978-1-57990-987-1
ISBN 10: 1-57990-987-6

For information about custom editions, special sales, premium and
corporate purchases, please contact Sterling Special Sales Department
at 800-805-5489 or specialsales@sterlingpub.com.

Table of Contents

Introduction

Those who view my paper stitching work might describe it as energetic and dynamic. When I discovered stitching on paper, however, the driving factor was actually not very interesting—I wanted to make sure my scrapbook pages wouldn't fall apart. But, as stitching began creeping its way into all aspects of my pages, I found that it enhanced them, adding depth, texture, and personality.

No matter what kind of crafter you are, you will find that sewing on paper adds another dimension, another texture, and a unique look to your craft project. Quilters can use it to try stitching on a different medium. Knitters can put their fibers to use in a different way. Scrapbookers will discover that stitching on paper adds texture and dimension without adding bulk and heaviness, and collage artists will find it an interesting alternative to adhesives. Plus, paper stitching ensures longevity of the paper craft where many adhesives cannot make such a guarantee.

My personal love for stitching started early. As a child, I was intrigued by sewing, painting, type fonts, and all sorts of crafts. Thankfully, my mother indulged my love of fabric and threads by providing me with projects. She was always by my side encouraging me and has always believed in my creativity.

As an adult, I discovered that I had a particular love for working with paper. My journey toward paper stitching didn't start until 2002, however, when I attended a workshop taught by Susan Carlson, author of *Free-Style Quilts: A No Rules Approach*. She taught us a wonderful technique in which art quilts are made from scraps of fabric and found objects, as well as how to piece together fabric scraps to resemble a photograph. Somehow, thanks to my newfound passion for paper, I couldn't get motivated to use just fabrics. I was beginning to delve heavily into the world of scrapbooking at the time, and I began to wonder how I could incorporate quilting techniques like stitches into my pages. My free-style quilt then became a free-style scrapbook page. "Crazy Fish," opposite, was complete and my love for off-kilter, lively stitching began.

As you read through and use this book, I hope that you feel empowered and inspired to create great works of art yourself. Observe how I use stitching in my projects—by both hand and machine—and use the techniques as a catalyst for new and unique ideas of your own. Even if you have never sewn before, I encourage you to try stitching on paper, have fun with it, and add your own personality and style.

This book will give you information about the fibers and tools required to stitch on paper projects and about how to incorporate traditional quilting and sewing techniques in projects. You will also learn standard hand and embroidery stitches and find 60 projects for inspiration. While the book contains several techniques, some of which are advanced, anyone with even a little bit of sewing knowledge should feel comfortable incorporating stitching in his or her paper projects.

I hope you will become as motivated as I am to create art scrapbooks that will last a lifetime and that showcase your signature style. Simply follow along with me on your journey to master the techniques found throughout this book. If you can stitch on fabric, you can stitch on paper. It's that simple.

Chapter 1

The Basics

Your scrapbook sewing kit is just like a toolbox. It should always be filled with the right tools and supplies to complete each piece. This chapter tells you exactly what you need and how to use it to achieve whatever look you want.

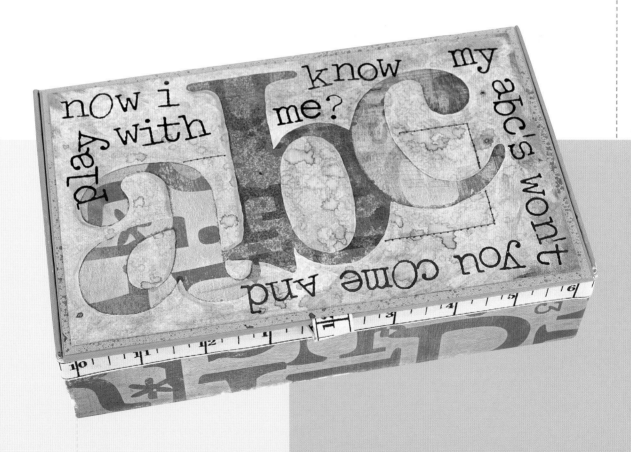

Tools to Stitch With

Having the proper tools to remodel a room is part of a carpenter's job. Generally, you see a carpenter arrive with a toolbox filled with replacement saw blades, hammers, nails, and whatever else he needs to get the job done. When working on a paper sewing project, the right tools are just as important.

Some of my favorite tools to use when hand stitching on my paper projects can be found at your local scrapbook or craft store. Others can be found by simply looking through your sewing box.

Acrylic Stitch Template: Stitching templates make hole placement fairly simple, and there are many available on the market. Templates are useful when time is short. Simply place the template over the spot that will be stitched, and use the piercing tool to make the holes. When I want to be especially careful with stitch placement, I plan the path I want the stitches to follow and mark the holes with a pencil before piercing. On those occasions that I cannot find the desired template, I find it easy to create my own. Refer to the Embroidery Stitch Template instructions on this page.

Needles: I prefer needles that are long and easy to thread; however any type of needle will work.

Paper Piercing Tool: There are various styles available on the market. Some are fairly basic and do just the intended job—pierce holes in the paper. Others have a needle threader and needle storage built into them. While these are great options to have, simply having a sharp tool to pierce a tiny hole through the paper will work.

Push Pad: The cushiony surface of the pad protects your work surface, provides the needle with some padding, and aids in creating a clean, uniform hole for stitching. Simply place the paper on top of the pad and pierce holes in the desired areas.

Plastic Alphabet Stencil: This tool makes stitching titles and alphabet accents quick and easy.

Scissors: When trimming threads, the smaller and sharper the better; however, any scissors will suffice.

Seam Ripper: Mistakes can easily be fixed with this handy little tool that will remove stitches without damaging the paper.

Sewing Machine: Any sewing machine with which you are comfortable will do. I highly recommend practicing with scrap paper and duplicate photos to become comfortable with the process before working on a treasured scrapbook page.

Embroidery Stitch Templates

If you have a specific pattern or motif that you would like to stitch, making your own template is easy. Simply follow these easy instructions.

Materials

Hammer

Paper punch, $\frac{1}{16}$" diameter

Pattern

Pencil

Stencil plastic, heavy chipboard, or thick plastic (such as a whipped topping lid)

Instructions

1. Transfer the desired pattern to the plastic or chipboard. This can be done freehand or by using carbon transfer paper.

2. Pencil in dots along the outline of the pattern, approximately $\frac{1}{4}$"–$\frac{3}{8}$" apart.

3. Punch a hole at each dot.

4. Repeat until all holes have been punched.

(Clockwise from top right) Push pad, scissors, craft needles, plastic alphabet stencils, seam ripper, paper piercing tool (silver), and acrylic stitch template.

Craft Needles

Fibers & Threads

The fibers or threads chosen for stitching on paper-crafted projects can literally make or break the piece. Using leather or twine on delicate paper is not reasonable, as the paper will likely tear before the stitching is finished. However, reinforcing delicate paper with a heavy-duty cardstock or fabric interfacing can be a fine solution, as can reaching for fine cotton Percale thread. If choosing the latter option, make certain to pierce a hole large enough to accommodate the needle and thread.

All-purpose Dual Duty Mercerized Cotton: This is my thread of choice for my sewing machine. It's easy to find, comes in a wide variety of colors and is fairly inexpensive. This thread also works well for hand stitching delicate designs.

Cotton Perle Thread: Cotton Perle thread has a wonderful texture and comes in a variety of colors. Typically used for embroidery or Hardanger, it is great to use on scrapbook pages as it stands up to repeated stitching through the holes and doesn't lose texture or shape. Cotton Perle is my favorite thread to hand stitch with.

Embroidery Floss: Embroidery floss comes in hundreds of colors and is unique in that it has six strands. It can be used as is or separated for more delicate stitching. Try using one strand from two or three different colors for a unique look.

Yarns: Hand stitching with any type of yarn is simple; however, make certain the dyes are acid-free if that is a concern for you. Natural or man-made fibers will work nicely on any scrapbook page or project. Yarns and thick fibers come in such a wide array of colors that it is practically impossible not to find something that matches any given project. Working with yarn is much like working with embroidery floss, although it may be necessary to pierce a larger hole for yarn to prevent the paper from tearing.

Tip:

Thicker fibers or yarns may require larger holes pierced in the paper. Make certain to pierce the holes far enough away from each other, as those that are too close together have a tendency to tear, while the fibers will create rough edges around holes that are too small.

All-purpose dual-duty mercerized cotton

(Clockwise from top right)
Cotton Perle thread, embroidery
floss, and wool yarn.

More Fibers & Threads

Leather: Leather is easy to work with and adds flair to any scrapbook page. Although it is available in a limited range of colors, a bit of acrylic paint will make it match the rest of the project quite nicely. Some leather cording may require the use of a paper punch, as it may be too large for standard hole piercing methods. Simply reinforce each hole with an eyelet before threading the leather through to prevent the paper from tearing.

Linen Thread: Linen thread is most often used in making lace, but in the paper industry it is used for bookbinding because of its strength. This fiber is a great choice when hand stitching or incorporating embroidery stitches in handmade books or scrapbook pages. I like to use linen thread in its natural state—un-dyed and free of any wax. The fiber is all-natural and should last a lifetime.

Novelty Yarns: Today's yarns include a wide variety of novelty yarns in many colors and textures. You can add drama and flair to a project with fluffy eyelash yarn, fuzzy metallic yarn, thick chenille yarn, nubby wool, and much more. Most novelty yarns will require you to punch larger holes in the paper to compensate for their thickness and unique textures. Use a paper punch to create the holes.

Paper Floss: Paper floss is a fairly new product that can be used just like twine or embroidery thread. It is actually made from paper and is acid- and lignin-free.

Twine and Hemp Twine: Because twine is so easy to work with and quite affordable, I often find myself reaching for it when working on a project. Twine works especially well with earthy colors and country- or outdoor-themed projects. Like leather, its range of colors is limited, but you can fix that with a little paint.

Hemp is an extremely strong fiber and is another natural textile to use in projects. It is stiff enough to hand stitch without using a needle. Widely available and inexpensive, hemp is easy to "color" as well. Simply hold the fiber directly on an inkpad and draw the length of the fiber over the pad. Repeat until you have reached the desired color.

Waxed Thread: This fiber is linen thread coated in wax. You can use it with a large needle, but it also works well when stitching without a needle because the wax allows the linen to keep its shape as you weave in and out of the holes you have pierced. Waxed thread also works well for securing charms, buttons, and beads to projects. Because the natural color of the linen is light, you will often find it dyed in a large assortment of colors. Be certain you know the ply when ordering waxed thread over the Internet; it comes in a variety of thicknesses, and depending on the type of project the thread may be too thick or too thin. The sizes range from 2- to 12-ply.

Tip:

You can easily make your own waxed thread. First, melt some beeswax. (Just a small amount is necessary.) Drag linen fiber through the hot melted wax, and then let it cool. Be careful not to burn yourself.

(Clockwise from top) Leather cord, novelty yarns, all-purpose dual duty mercerized cotton, waxed thread (black and blue), twine (brown), and linen thread (white).

17

Hand Stitch Examples

Blanket Stitch

I find this stitch works best when used for its original intention—to create a border. If using around the edge of a page, punch one row of holes approximately ¼"–½" from the edge of the paper. To use this stitch away from the edge, punch two parallel lines of holes around the item being stitched.

1. Bring the thread out on the lower line and insert the needle in position in the upper line, taking a straight downward stitch with the thread under the needle point. *Note: If using this technique as a border, simply loop the thread around the edge of the page instead of working between two sets of holes.*

2. Pull up the stitch to form a loop and repeat.

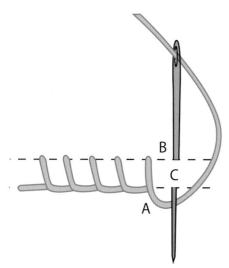

Back Stitch

This stitch works well with titles or as a simple border to emphasize a spot in a certain photograph.

1. Bring the thread through on the stitch line, then take a small backward stitch through the paper.

2. Bring the needle through again a little in front

of the first stitch. Take another stitch, inserting the needle at the point where it first came through.

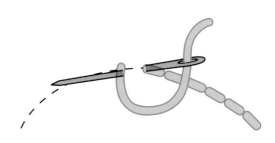

Straight Stitch

This simple stitch is easy to do and works well for minimalist pages, as it won't detract from the rest of the page.

1. Pass the needle over and under the paper, making the upper stitches of equal length.

2. Make the under stitches of equal length as well, but half the size, or less, of the upper stitches.

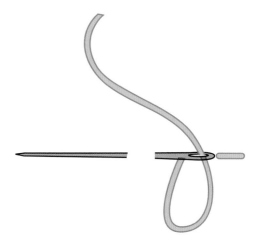

Herringbone Stitch

This stitch makes a beautiful border and, once learned, is very simple to complete. It can often replace photo corners if using a template. Simply pierce two parallel lines of holes in the desired area, referring to the diagram as necessary.

1. Bring the needle out on the lower left-hand side, and insert on the upper line, one hole to the right. Bring the needle back out through the hole directly to the left, referring to diagram. Make certain to keep the thread below the needle.

2. Insert the needle on the lower line slightly to the right, and take a small stitch to the left with the thread above the needle.

3. Repeat these two movements throughout.

French Knot

This little detail will add subtle personality to your pages.

1. Bring the thread out at the required position. Hold the thread down with the left thumb and encircle the thread twice with the needle as shown.

2. Holding the thread firmly, twist the needle back to the starting point and insert near the spot at which the thread first emerged.

3. Pull thread through to the back and secure for a single French knot, or pass on to the position of the next stitch.

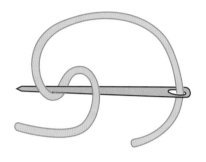

It's easy to add titles and other text to your project using alphabet and number templates. Templates can easily be created using a favorite computer font to add personality and interest to your pages.

The Internet is a wonderful resource to find new and free fonts. It is easy to locate free download sites and browse through the thousands of fonts available. Once a font is downloaded and installed, it's like having a new set of alphabet stamps.

1. Making certain that text is of the desired font and size, print page title/wording in light grey on bond paper.

2. Using a pencil, mark each letter where the holes will be pierced for the stitching.

3. Pierce holes through the project surface along the outline of the letter, where indicated by the pencil marks.

4. Stitch with the desired thread or fiber.

Alphabet Template

1. Follow Steps 1–2 of the instructions above.

2. Spray the back of the paper with adhesive and mount to thick stencil plastic.

3. Using a hammer and ¹⁄₁₆" eyelet maker, punch the holes along the outline of each letter.

Tip:

Rounded corners will need shorter stitches to complement the shape of the letter. To keep stitch size consistent, you can make shorter stitches all the way around the letter, or the stitch sizes can be varied, remaining longer on the straight edges and shorter when the letter rounds.

Machine Stitching Tips and Tricks

When stitching with a sewing machine, keep the following tips and tricks in mind.

- Each time you change the bobbin or top thread, make certain to do several test stitches to ensure the machine is threaded correctly. This will help eliminate any problems while stitching on paper.

- I have found that the longer the stitch, the better the results. Using a small stitch will perforate the paper, causing it to fall apart. If you want to use an embroidery-type stitch, stitch on two or more pieces and sandwich interfacing between the papers to reinforce them and prevent perforation.

- Use as small a needle as possible so the holes will not be visible on the paper.

- Use small amounts of adhesive only in areas you are not planning to stitch. Adhesives have a tendency to gum up the needle and sewing machine as the needle pierces through it.

- To ensure sewing in the correct spot, lightly mark in the line with a pencil, then follow this line with the needle. It is not necessary to erase the line if it is light enough and has been sewn over directly.

- To secure the threads when finished stitching, pull the top thread to the back, tie the threads together, then clip.

- When nearing a corner, sew as slowly as possible—or one stitch at a time—to ensure being able to stop when desired. If you inadvertently pass the stopping point, backstitch until you reach the corner, then turn the paper.

- When using the zigzag stitch, move the width dial from straight to a wide stitch. This creates a "heart monitor" pattern that varies depending on the speed at which you are sewing.

Faux Stitching

If you love the look of stitching but don't have exactly what you need on hand, you can emulate the look with markers, acrylic stamps, and rub-ons. Rub-ons are my personal favorite for creating faux-stitched titles and words, and are available from several manufacturers. If it is difficult to find faux-stitch rub-ons, simply use a thin marker to create custom faux stitching across your page. Remember, it doesn't have to be perfect!

1. Refer to actual machine- or hand-stitched items in order to accurately duplicate the desired pattern.

2. If you are uncertain as to whether this is the desired look, use a fine-tipped marker to sketch the stitch onto a transparency. Lay the transparency over the area in which the faux stitching will be completed for a test run.

3. Lightly pencil the line or spot where the stitching will be added.

4. Lightly shadow around the penciled line with a fine-tip marker. *Note: This will add dimension to the stitches, much like machine- or hand-stitched pieces.*

5. Use rub-ons, stamps, or a non-bleeding pen to complete the faux stitching.

Tip:

Iron-on faux stitching is also available in many craft stores in the clothing embellishments section. It creates a great look and is quite easy to accomplish. Another way to create a stitched look without doing any sewing is to use a stapler. Simply load your stapler with colored staples and try using papers with a stitching pattern pre-printed on them. You can get the look of a stitched page quickly and easily.

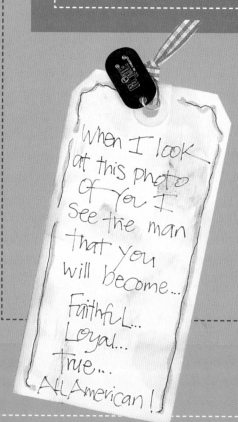

When I look at this photo of You I see the man that you will become... Faithful... Loyal... True... All American!

wonder · adventure · experience

play

CLAM

happiness

and dare to have fun

FLATS

discover

*These projects show examples
of faux stitching*

Cape DiSAPoinTMENT

A BEACON OF Light

Chapter 2

Stitching

Now that you've been introduced to the basics, it's time to put that knowledge down on paper, so to speak. The projects in this chapter will introduce you to all the ways you can use basic stitching in your scrapbook pages and paper projects.

Innocent Love

Materials

Acrylic paint

Adhesive

Alphabet stickers

Brad

Cardstock, textured

Color wash and spray bottle

Craft scissors

Inkpads

Iron and ironing board

Mailbox address number

Mercerized cotton thread

Paintbrush

Paper, patterned

Photographs

Photo turn

Rubber stamps

Sandpaper

Scrapbooking file folder, small

Sewing machine

Silk flowers

Wooden tag

Instructions

1. Trim patterned paper and photograph to desired size. Mat on coordinating cardstock.

2. Spritz file folder with color wash to match silk flowers. Swirl matching ink around to create a tie-dye effect. Allow to dry.

3. Iron file folder flat and attach stickers to outside. Stamp additional details as desired.

4. Place additional photographs inside the file folder and adhere folder to layout.

5. Sand and paint wooden tag. Allow to dry. Sand again to give it a distressed look and embellish with alphabet stickers. Adhere to layout.

6. Lightly adhere silk flowers around the layout. Create several French knots in the center of each flower. Refer to French Knot Instructions on page 19.

7. Sand reflective paint off the mailbox number and stitch to layout.

8. Machine stitch around the photograph and borders of the layout.

All Tom Girl

Materials

- Adhesive
- Beads
- Brads
- Cardstock, textured
- Chipboard flowers
- Color wash and spray bottle
- Craft scissors
- Double-stick tape
- Fabric alphabet
- Foam stamps
- Inkpads, desired colors
- Letter beads
- Paint
- Paper, patterned
- Photographs
- Silk ribbon
- Sponge

Instructions

1. Mount a 5" x 7" photograph onto cardstock and adhere to patterned paper.

2. Spritz chipboard shapes with color wash, then sponge with ink and allow to dry. Sponge again with a second color of ink. *Note: I used burgundy and orange ink, respectively, for my project.*

3. Adhere all photographs to layout as shown in photograph, or as desired.

4. Pierce a hole in the center of each flower with a paper piercer and attach to layout with a French knot. Refer to French Knot instructions on page 19.

5. Vary the centers of the flowers by randomly attaching letter beads and brads.

6. Attach fabric letters to layout with double-stick tape, then stitch, varying between a straight stitch and a zigzag stitch.

7. Foam stamp the word "Girl" as shown, or as desired.

8. Using a long straight stitch, stitch around the edges of the layout.

ALL

TOM

GirL

Fly Shadowbox Card

Materials

Acrylic paint

Adhesive

Chipboard letters

Clear stamps

Craft scissors

Double-stick tape

Inkpads

Mercerized cotton thread

Paintbrush

Paper, patterned

Ribbon

Ribbon slide

Rusty dragonfly charm

Shadowbox, 6"-square

Vellum flowers

Instructions

1. Trim patterned paper to fit shadowbox.

2. Cut random oblong shapes from several coordinating patterned papers and attach to patterned paper trimmed in Step 1 with double-stick tape.

3. Pierce holes along the seam of the paper in various patterns. *Note: The page in the photograph uses the herringbone stitch and a parallel straight stitch.*

4. Paint chipboard letters as desired and adhere to page. Reinforce with desired stitching.

5. Tie ribbon to metal dragonfly charm. Pierce holes in an X pattern and stitch the charm and ribbon to the page using Xs.

6. Stitch patterns with mercerized cotton.

7. Adhere flowers to page, then stitch French knots in the centers. Refer to French Knot Instructions on page 19.

8. Stamp additional words with clear stamps.

Deep Soul

Materials

Adhesive

Clear stamps, snowflakes

Cardstock, textured

Craft scissors

Inkpads, watermark and white

Marker, pen or desired
journaling utensil

Mercerized cotton thread

Needle

Ribbon

Sewing machine

Shipping tag

Watermark inkpad

Instructions

1. Stamp snowflake pattern in both inks onto the cardstock. Allow to dry.

2. Pierce holes in the snowflake pattern. Using the backstitch, hand stitch the pattern, following the pierced holes.

3. Adhere ribbon to page, then stitch into place.

4. Journal the manila tag with desired wording.

5. Machine stitch around the photograph, leaving the top open for the journaled tag to peek out.

G is the
hard
part!

gOOdbye

Chapter 3

Alphabets & Titles

I love the look of stitched titles and alphabet accents on my scrapbook pages. They add texture, depth, and a creative look to any paper project. The infinite selection of fonts you can use—from whimsical to elegant to modern—means infinite possibilities for your pages.

Knight in Shining Armor

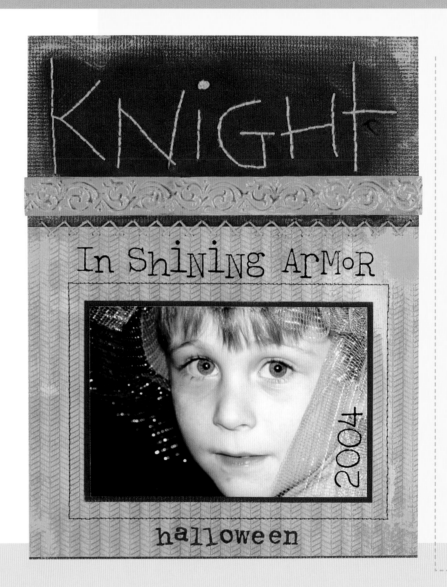

Materials

Acrylic paint

Adhesive

Bond paper

Cardstock, textured

Computer and printer

Craft scissors

Inkpads

Mercerized cotton thread

Needle

Paintbrush

Photograph

Rub-ons

Rubber stamps

Sandpaper

Self-adhesive molding strip

Sewing machine

Instructions

1. Refer to Stitching Alphabets & Titles on page 20 to create and use an alphabet template. Straight stitch using the pierced holes as a pattern.

2. Distress edges of paper by lightly rubbing sandpaper along the edges, then dry brush with acrylic paint. Allow to dry.

3. Layer and adhere patterned paper and photograph to layout. Machine stitch a border around the photograph.

4. Paint and sand metal molding strip. Adhere to page.

5. Embellish title with alphabet stamps and rub-ons.

Take Happiness

Materials

Acrylic letters

Adhesive

Brads

Cardstock matchbooks

Cardstock, textured

Computer and printer

Craft scissors

Fabric pens

Mercerized cotton thread

Needle

Printable self-adhesive fabric

Rub-on letters

Sewing machine

Silk flowers

Stickers

Yarn

Instructions

1. Print photograph on adhesive fabric, following printer user's manual. Allow to dry.

2. Hand-color with fabric pens, making certain to use a light hand, as the fabric pens will smear easily.

3. Adhere fabric to layout.

4. Machine quilt hand-colored portion of the fabric.

5. Pierce the letter "h" on the bottom of the layout, overlapping the fabric as shown in photograph. Hand-color the portion of the "h" that overlaps the fabric. Allow to dry.

6. Stitch the "h" with thread.

7. Apply rub-on letters as shown, or as desired.

8. Using brads, attach foldout cardstock matchbooks to page. Embellish with silk flowers, brads, and stickers.

9. Complete the last line of the quote underneath the last flap of the matchbooks using rub-ons, stitching, or as desired. *Note: The hidden journaling for this project says, "Put it in your soul."*

Easter Egg Hunt

Materials

Adhesive

Bond paper

Cardstock

Chicken template (optional)

Computer and printer

Craft scissors

Fabric, patterned

Marker, pen, or desired journaling utensil

Mercerized cotton thread

Needle

Paper, patterned

Pen, platinum

Repositionable adhesive

Instructions

1. Create title in word processing program and print on bond paper.

2. Trim cardstock to desired size.

3. Adhere title to cardstock with repositionable adhesive.

4. Pierce holes in each of the title letters.

5. Outline each letter with the platinum pen. *Note: This will give the title a three-dimensional effect once the project is complete.*

6. Stitch the title using a straight stitch. Refer to Straight Stitch Instructions on page 18.

7. Adhere cardstock to patterned paper, stitching on a herringbone border. Refer to Herringbone Stitch Instructions on page 19.

8. Cut chickens from patterned fabric and attach to the page. Add legs or feet, if desired. *Note: I cut my chickens freehand. If you are not comfortable with this, purchase a template from the craft or scrapbooking store.*

9. Crazy stitch around the center of some of the chickens and straight stitch around the borders of others.

10. Mat photographs on cardstock and stitch to layout using a varying pattern of stitches.

11. Hand journal desired wording onto layout.

easter
egg hunt

April, 2001 - You were so cute to watch as you searched
Gram's yard for Easter eggs. You were a little over 2 and
a half this Easter - old enough to find the eggs and put
them in the basket - but not old enough to get excited
over the thought of a bunny leaving candy in an egg
around the yard for you to find. I loved watching you run
around the yard putting eggs in your
basket.

Sweet Dreams

Materials

Acrylic paint

Adhesive

Cardstock, textured

Chipboard letters

Computer with photo-editing program and printer

Mercerized cotton thread

Needle

Paintbrush

Paper, patterned

Pencil

Pen, platinum

Photo corners, large

Photo mat

Prepared canvas

Rub-on letters

Sewing machine

Instructions

1. Manipulate photograph in a photo-editing program to resemble a watercolor painting.

2. Print photograph on prepared canvas, referring to printer owner's manual.

3. Tear the excess white space from the canvas so that the edges are frayed.

4. Adhere patterned paper to cardstock, then zigzag stitch around three of the edges with a stitch length of 3 and a stitch width of 2 so that a wavy look is achieved.

5. Adhere matted patterned paper to layout using photo corners, then machine straight stitch around the edges.

6. Mount canvas onto photo mat and crazy stitch around the edges, making certain not to stitch over any important areas of the photograph.

7. Print the word "Dreams" in a decorative font onto scrap paper. Transfer to patterned paper with a light pencil mark.

8. Mat patterned paper onto layout. Pierce hole on the light pencil lines, then hand stitch the title using a straight stitch.

9. Create a shadow with platinum pen.

10. Paint chipboard letters and allow to dry.

11. Adhere chipboard letters as desired and hand stitch for added security.

12. Machine stitch around title. Embellish with rub-on letters.

an early morn... SWEET Dreams... cAught In mY heArt

Saying Goodbye

Materials

Adhesive

Cardstock, textured white

Chipboard

Chipboard shapes

Craft scissors

Mercerized cotton thread

Paper, patterned

Pencil

Photographs

Ribbon

Rub-on letters

Shipping tag

Twill

Walnut ink or dye and spray bottle

Instructions

1. Cut desired letter from paper or chipboard.

2. Place on small piece of cardstock and spritz with walnut ink or dye. Allow to dry.

3. Discard letter.

4. Lightly pencil lines around the perimeter of the letter on the cardstock and pierce evenly-spaced holes for hand stitching. Varying between stitch types, hand stitch within the letter to create a pattern.

5. Adhere cardstock with hand-stitched letter to layout, then stitch using coordinating thread.

6. Mat large photograph as desired and stitch to layout, leaving an opening at the top to create a journaling pocket.

7. Adhere other photographs to layout, then stitch into place.

8. Embellish with ribbons, rub-ons, and chipboard elements.

9. Journal desired wording onto shipping tag and insert into pocket.

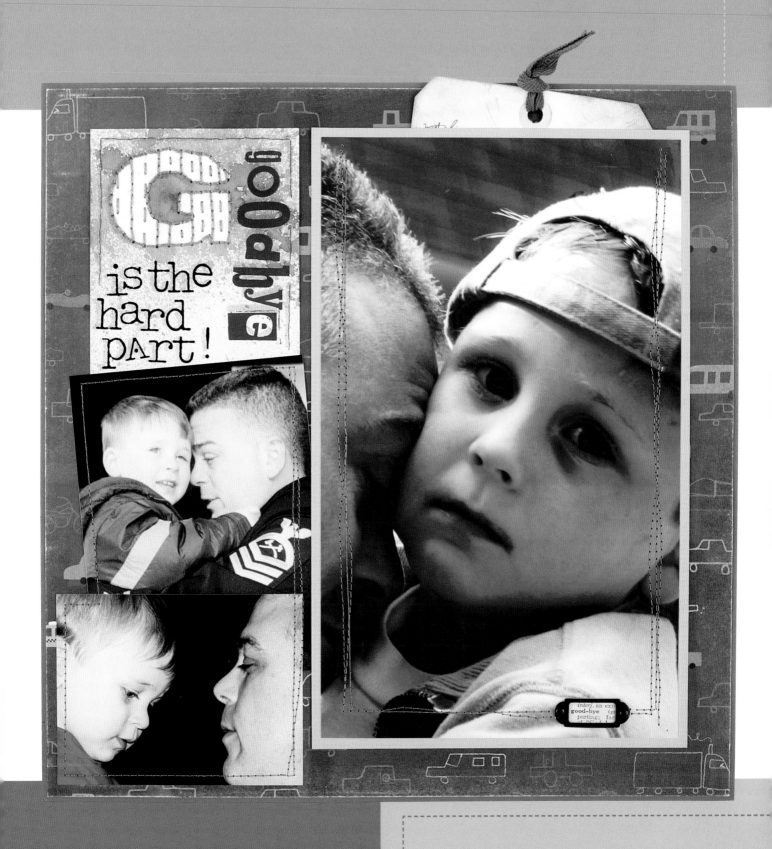

GOODBYE

is the
hard
PARt!

goodbye

mom   artist   me   wife

CREATE

imagine   inspire   believe   create   dream   ho

I Am all
ThaT — &
SO MuCH
MORE!

Chapter 4

Faux Stitching & Embellishing

Sometimes a scrapbook page or paper project needs a little something to give it extra panache. Stitching is a secure way to embellish your projects with trims, ephemera, beads, buttons, charms, and found objects. Or, if you prefer, quickly and easily add faux stitching to a page. Whether you use silk flowers or rub-on stitches, embellishments will give your pages appealing texture, dimension, and style.

Sea Shells by the Sea

Materials

Acid-free glue stick

Acrylic paint

Adhesive

Antique findings

Canvas, 6"-square (2)

Chipboard shapes

Clear glaze

Computer and laser printer

Cotton Perle thread

Embossing ink

Embossing powder

Glue stick

Heat gun

Inkpads

Measuring tape (optional)

Metallic cream paint

Needle

Paintbrush

Paper, patterned

Pencil

Ribbons: antique and velvet

Rub-on letters

Soft plastic washers

Sponge

Stretcher bar

Upholstery tacks

Instructions

1. Following stretcher bar package directions, stretch canvas to fit.

2. Sponge ink and paint canvas squares until desired color is achieved. Allow to dry.

3. Back stitch a square following the inner edge of the stretcher bar on the back of the canvas.

4. Lightly pencil a spiral inside the box. Varying between colors, stitch the spiral.

5. Sponge ink onto soft plastic washers, then spray with clear glaze and allow to dry.

6. Attach antique ribbon or measuring tape onto the canvas using upholstery tacks as shown in photograph, or as desired.

7. Print photograph using a laser printer. Using glue stick, mat onto patterned paper and allow to dry.

8. Rub embossing ink over the photograph and coat with embossing powder. Heat with a heat gun.

9. Repeat Step 8 until desired thickness has been achieved.

10. Attach photograph to canvas using upholstery tacks.

11. Embellish project with velvet ribbon, antique findings, and chipboard shapes.

Who Am I? Discovery Folio

Materials

Acrylic paint

Adhesive

Cardstock, textured

Charms

Craft scissors

Die-cut tags

Mercerized cotton thread

Metal embellishment tags

Paper, patterned

Paintbrush

Photographs

Ribbon

Scrapbooking file folder, small

Self-adhesive zipper

Sewing machine

Shipping tags

Silk leaves

Twill

Twine

Wooden tag

Instructions

1. Trim a sheet of patterned paper to 11" x 8½".

2. Trim a second sheet of coordinating patterned paper to 11" x 7". Machine stitch zipper to the long side of the paper.

3. Place the smaller sheet on top of the larger sheet. Trim a sheet of patterned paper to fit the space over the zipper, creating a folio.

4. Using your sewing machine, zigzag stitch around the perimeter of the folio.

5. Paint wooden tag and allow to dry.

6. Embellish outside of folio with twill, twine, leaves, and lettering, or as desired. Attach painted wooden tag to folio using adhesive or twine, or as desired.

7. Cut sheets of cardstock to resemble file folders with half-circle tabs at the top, as shown in photograph.

8. Embellish cardstock sheets with patterned papers, photographs, and journaled shipping tags, as desired.

Tip:

Use this fun folio to keep favorite quotes, ticket stubs, and other memorabilia safe while collecting information for that "All About Me" scrapbook you've been wanting to start.

mom artist me wife

imagine inspire INSPIRE who Am I? ho

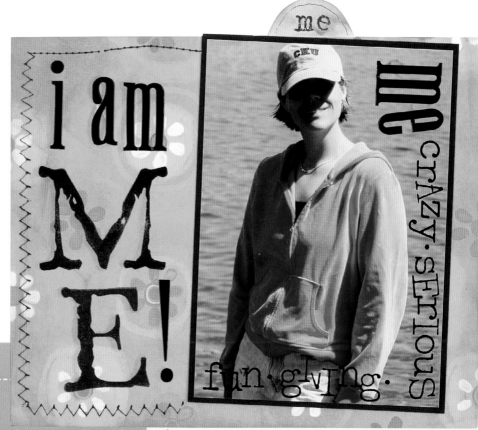

me

i am M E!

me crazy.serious. fun.giving.

47

Sitting on the Porch Step

Materials

Adhesive

Cardstock stickers

Cardstock, textured

Chalk

Craft scissors

Inkpads

Journaling cards or tags

Marker, pen, or desired journaling utensil

Mercerized cotton thread

Metal letters

Paper, patterned

Removable tape

Rubber stamps

Sewing machine

Stickers

Yarn

Instructions

1. Trim cardstock to desired size.

2. Stamp title onto cardstock and adhere metal letters, embellishing as desired.

3. Tear cardstock for pocket to desired size and embellish with stickers and yarn, as desired.

4. Chalk pocket edges. Use removable tape to temporarily attach pocket to layout. *Note: This makes it much easier for the pocket to remain in place while machine stitching.* Machine stitch sides and bottom of pocket into place.

5. Layer and adhere patterned paper to cardstock. Embellish with ribbons and secure with machine stitching.

6. Journal cards or tags and insert into pocket.

Spencer

Materials

Acrylic paint

Adhesive

Cardstock, textured

Charm

Craft scissors

Die-cut dog stickers

Foam stamps

Mercerized cotton thread

Paper, dog patterned

Ribbon, velvet

Sewing machine

Translucent vellum sheet, 12"
-square with dog phrases

Instructions

1. Trim patterned paper to desired size and stamp title using foam stamps and acrylic paint.

2. Adhere to cardstock.

3. Mount photograph onto cardstock, then layer and adhere to patterned paper.

4. Embellish layout with ribbon and charm. *Note: Ribbon can be adhered with glue and then stitched when dry for added detail as well as reinforcement.*

5. Zigzag stitch photograph on three sides, or as desired.

Scanlon Family

Materials

Adhesive

Cardstock, textured

Color wash

Craft scissors

Foam stamps

Inkpads

Mercerized cotton thread

Paper flowers

Paper, handmade and patterned

Rub-on letters

Sewing machine

Shipping tag

Instructions

1. Trim patterned paper to desired size and stamp title in desired area.

2. Adhere to cardstock.

3. Double-mat photographs onto coordinating cardstock and handmade paper. Adhere to patterned paper as shown in photograph, or as desired.

4. Zigzag stitch around photo on sides and bottom. Make certain to leave the top open to create a pocket for shipping tag journaling card.

5. Following package directions, dye tag using color wash to match page and allow to dry. Add desired journaling.

6. Cut a small strip of cardstock and staple to tag to function as pull-tab. Insert tag into pocket.

7. Embellish page by adhering paper flowers and adding rub-on letters.

Fall Frolic

Materials

Acrylic paint, gold

Adhesive

Aluminum foil

Cardstock, textured

Craft scissors

Date stamp

Dictionary definition

Disposable cup

Inkpad

Mercerized cotton thread

Paper alphabet squares

Raffia/acrylic paint custom paper kit

Ribbon

Sewing machine

Spoon

Instructions

1. Preheat oven to 150°F.

2. Mix one or two tablespoons gold paint with paper fiber paint from custom paper kit in disposable cup. *Note: It may be necessary to adjust the amount of paint used depending on the color desired.*

3. Randomly arrange desired amount of raffia on sheet of aluminum foil. Spread a thin coat of gold paint mixture over raffia.

4. Place in oven for 60 minutes to help eliminate some of the moisture. Set out on counter until thoroughly dry.

5. Mat custom paper to patterned paper and trim to desired size. Layer and adhere to cardstock and a second sheet of patterned paper.

6. Stitch to layout using desired stitching. *Note: I stitched my page with a random, circular, crazy stitch.*

7. Adhere photographs, dictionary definition, and ribbon to page. Secure them by machine stitching into place.

8. Adhere alphabet squares, if desired, before hand stitching into place.

9. Stamp date in desired area.

FALL

FROLIC

Love Is Patient

Materials

- Adhesive
- Alphabet stickers
- Cardstock: patterned, textured
- Computer and inkjet printer
- Digital photograph
- Double-stick tape
- Dragonfly charms
- Eyelet setter
- Eyelets
- Inkpad
- Iron and ironing board
- Iron-on transfer sheet
- Mercerized cotton thread
- Muslin with tattered edges
- Paper, patterned
- Scissors
- Sewing machine
- Small photograph
- Tag
- Transparency
- Waxed linen thread
- Word stamps

Instructions

1. Trim the textured cardstock to desired size. Adhere to the patterned cardstock.

2. Trim the patterned paper to desired size. Adhere to the page.

3. Print the digital photograph onto the iron-on transfer sheet according to printer user's manual. Iron to the muslin.

4. Stitch the muslin to the patterned paper around the photograph several times using a wavy stitch.

5. Mat the small photograph onto cardstock and adhere to the page.

6. Print the title and text onto the transparency. Using double-stick tape, adhere the transparency to the page, centering text as desired.

7. Stamp words onto a strip of cardstock and adhere to the page.

8. Adhere alphabet stickers to the tag.

9. Cut two thin strips of cardstock. Thread a cardstock strip through the tag. Using waxed linen thread, tie a dragonfly charm to the tag. Using double-stick tape, adhere the tag and cardstock strip to the page.

10. Set two eyelets in the remaining cardstock strip. Using waxed linen thread, tie the remaining dragonfly charm to the strip through the eyelets. Using double-stick tape, adhere the strip to the page.

11. Vary the stitches around the layout from straight to zigzag.

Tip:

Varying stitches is easy to do. It is a fun technique to try at a medium speed. Set the knob to zigzag and adjust the stitch width from straight to wide. Just move the width slider back and forth.

love is patient

love is kind and envies no one.
Love is never boastful, nor conceited,
nor rude; never selfish,
not quick to take offense.
There is nothing love cannot face;
there is no limit to its faith,
its hope, and endurance.
In a word, there are three things
that last forever: faith, hope, and love;
but the greatest of them all is love.

~ 1 Corinthians 13

FAITH ❀ HOPE ❀ LOVE

C & J

Cape Disappointment: A Beacon of Light

Materials

Adhesive

Brads

Cardstock, textured

Clear stamps

Craft scissors

Inkpad, blue

Marker, pen, or desired journaling utensil

Metal alphabet charms

Paper, patterned

Photographs

Ribbon

Rub-on stitches

Shipping tag

Stapler

Water crayons

Instructions

1. Trim patterned paper and mat on cardstock.

2. Mount 8" x 10" photograph to cardstock. Hand-color with water crayons.

3. Create title for page by alternating between rub-on letters and metal alphabet charm.

4. Apply rub-ons to create an emulated machine-stitched border.

5. Add mini-photographs and 3½" x 5" close-up.

6. Journal desired wording onto tag. Staple ribbon to top and slip tag behind largest photograph.

Clam Flats

Materials

Acrylic paint

Adhesive

Cardstock, textured

Craft scissors

Fabric strips

Foam stamps

Inkpads

Metal tag

Paintbrush

Paper, patterned

Photographs, black-and-white

Rub-ons: stitches and words

Twine

Instructions

1. Using foam stamps, acrylic paint, and rub-on words, create title on a strip of patterned paper of desired size.

2. Mat onto cardstock and adhere a black-and-white photograph to top.

3. Mat a piece of patterned paper to cardstock and dry brush the edges with acrylic paint. Allow to dry.

4. Adhere two black-and-white photographs to patterned paper. Add rub-on stitches to two edges of each photo.

5. Mat title strip to layout.

6. Embellish with metal tag, twine, and ribbons as desired.

a Visit To the

Pumpkin Farm

Chapter 5

Machine Stitching

Using a sewing machine is a great way to add a variety of stitches to your projects in a fraction of the time it would take to hand stitch them. Today's sewing machines are more user-friendly than ever and contain dozens of interesting stitches. Practice on scrap paper first to try your hand and to preview the look of a particular stitch. Then use your new skills to start adding even more character to your pages.

Bode

Materials

Acrylic paint

Adhesive

Cardstock, textured

Craft scissors

Fabric paper sheets

Mercerized cotton thread

Metallic thread

Needle

Paintbrush

Photographs

Sewing machine

Wooden letter

Instructions

1. Trim fabric paper and mat onto cardstock.

2. Adhere small photographs to cardstock, with top edges tucked beneath the edge of the fabric paper as shown in photograph.

3. Use the metallic thread to stitch desired border. Machine quilt the center of the layout.

4. Adhere large photo to fabric paper, adding a stitched border around it.

5. Paint wooden letter and allow to dry.

6. Hand stitch letter to layout as shown, or as desired.

Tip:

Heavily starched fabric sheets that resemble paper can be purchased at your local craft store, or online. The patterns printed on these fabric sheets are great and a paper trimmer works well for cutting through them.

Wiener Dog

Materials

- Adhesive
- Cardstock, textured
- Charm
- Craft scissors
- Mercerized cotton thread
- Paper, newsprint and patterned
- Ribbon
- Sewing machine
- Stickers
- Twine

Instructions

1. Trim patterned paper and adhere to cardstock.

2. Cut strips of newsprint paper and lay at an angle over the patterned paper.

3. Stitch around the perimeter of the entire 12"-square page.

4. Double-mat photographs and adhere to layout.

5. Stitch around the edges of two of the photographs. *Note: I stitched right on my photographs for added interest, but only at the top and in the backgrounds.*

6. Embellish page by adhering or stitching ribbon, charm, twill, and stickers as desired.

A Visit to the Pumpkin Farm

Materials

Acrylic paint

Adhesive

Brads

Chipboard frames (3)

Computer and printer with photo-editing program

Craft scissors

Foam stamps

Iron and ironing board

Mercerized cotton thread

Muslin

Paintbrush

Paper: handmade textured, patterned

Photographs

Rub-on letters

Sewing machine

Twill

Walnut ink

Instructions

1. Type a 300 pt. "P"(or whatever the first letter of your title is) in a photo-editing program. Overlap "P" with random words of choice in white or other color that will stand out, using a script font.

2. Print "P" onto muslin, referring to printer user's manual.

3. Heat-set the fabric by pressing with a hot iron for 10–15 seconds. Make certain not to scorch the muslin.

4. Tear the edges of the muslin until it is of desired size. Lightly brush the area surrounding the "P" with walnut ink to give the muslin an antiqued look.

5. Trim patterned paper to desired size.

6. Adhere patterned paper to handmade textured paper. Machine stitch around the edges using a zigzag stitch, sliding the width adjustment control slowly while stitching.

7. Adhere the muslin monogram to layout and zigzag in a random pattern around the edges.

8. Foam stamp title to page with coordinating acrylic paint color.

9. Tie twill around one photograph. Adhere three photographs to top of page as shown, or as desired.

10. Machine stitch around the edges of the center photograph. Adhere or stitch two chipboard frames to accentuate desired portions of photograph.

11. Finish title using rub-on letters.

12. Stitch around the edges of the last chipboard frame, then adhere to layout. Secure frame to layout by stitching with natural twine.

a Visit To the

Pumpkin farm

Best

Materials

Acrylic paint

Adhesive

Brads

Cardstock, textured

Craft scissors

Inkpad or bottled ink

Mercerized cotton thread

Metal frame, circular

Metal words

Paintbrush

Paper, patterned

Pencil

Photographs

Ruler

Self-adhesive embellishing tabs

Sewing machine

Silk flower

Twill

Instructions

1. Tear two pieces of cardstock to desired sizes and mat to patterned paper as shown in photograph. Wet and crumple, if desired.

2. Measure and lightly pencil a ¾" border around the top, right-hand side, and bottom edges of the layout.

3. Machine stitch the penciled border using a straight stitch. Switching to zigzag stitch, create a second border parallel to the first, as shown.

4. Adhere a large photograph to the center of the layout and stitch around the edges.

5. Overlap one edge of the photograph with a length of thin twill and zigzag stitch to secure them together.

6. Paint metal words or phrases and allow to dry.

7. Stitch metal words to layout as desired.

8. Machine stitch a small photograph to a small piece of cardstock. Stitch to the front of the layout as shown, leaving one edge open to create a pocket for hidden journaling.

9. Place self-adhesive embellishing tabs as shown, or as desired.

10. Remove the center from a silk flower. Adhere metal frame to flower's center.

11. Pierce holes in the frame's center and insert brads.

12. Color the center of the flower with ink.

ian, brooke and bode - three musketeers - the three amigos - cousins and friends too - like brothers and sister, like your uncle jeff, uncle ian and me, close in age - and close in spirit, i hope that you grow to be good friends, live near each other in the neighborhood and rely on each other like siblings do, like friends do,

American

Materials

- Acrylic paint
- Adhesive
- Cardstock: blue textured, red
- Chipboard letters
- Decorative tape
- Mercerized cotton thread
- Metal charm
- Needle
- Paintbrush
- Paper piercing tool
- Paper: blue patterned, yellow patterned
- Pencil
- Photographs
- Ribbon
- Scissors
- Sewing machine
- Shipping tag with journaling
- Toy dog tag

Instructions

1. Paint chipboard letters for title. Allow to dry.
2. Trim the yellow patterned paper to the desired size and adhere to blue textured cardstock.
3. Place adhesive along the bottom of a wide strip of blue patterned paper and adhere to the page. *Note: The top stays open to create a pocket for journaling.*
4. Double-mat photograph onto red cardstock and blue patterned paper. Adhere matted photograph and additional photographs to the page.
5. Embellish the page with tags, ribbon, decorative tape, and the metal charm.
6. Adhere chipboard letters for the title, leaving a space for the hand-stitched letter.
7. To create the hand-stitched letter, trace the coordinating chipboard letter onto the desired area. Pierce holes along the traced outline.
8. Stitch the letter.
9. Machine stitch around the photographs.
10. Using ribbon, tie the toy dog tag to the shipping tag. Place the tag inside the pocket.

Tip:

To create texture and variation on the page, try inserting an embroidered or straight-stitched alphabet in the title. It's an interesting detail that is simple and easy to complete.

Blizzard of 2005

Materials

- Acrylic paint
- Adhesive
- Brads
- Cardstock, green textured and white textured
- Craft scissors
- Foam stamps, alphabet
- Inkpads or bottled ink
- Mercerized cotton thread
- Paper, patterned
- Photographs
- Ribbon
- Sandpaper
- Sewing machine
- Tin letters
- Tin snowflake embellishments
- Twill

Instructions

1. Mat two wallet-size photographs on white cardstock and adhere to a strip of patterned paper. Mat patterned paper on to green cardstock and adhere to a 12"-square sheet of patterned paper.

2. Stitch a piece of ribbon to the top of the patterned paper strip on the layout.

3. Foam stamp the word "snow" on the bottom edge of the strip.

4. Double-mat an 8" x 10" photograph on green cardstock, then again on white cardstock. Adhere to layout as shown in photograph. Stitch around the top and sides of the photograph.

5. Attach ribbon and snowflake embellishments using brads.

6. Sand and ink tin letters to match snowflakes. Adhere directly to photograph as shown.

<sub>blizzard (bliz'ärd), n. a furious hurricane
of wind with fine blinding snow, and
characterized by intense cold; a dis-
charge of shots; a poser.</sub>

celebrate

BLIZZARD OF 2005

SNOW

You ARE

Materials

Adhesive or double-stick tape

Cardstock: brown, light blue

Craft scissors

Inkpad, blue

Mercerized cotton thread

Paper, brown patterned

Printed twill

Rubber stamps, alphabet

Rub-on letters

Sewing machine

Sponge

Instructions

1. Lightly sponge ink onto the edges and center of a sheet of cardstock.

2. Repeat Step 1 on a sheet of patterned paper and mount onto cardstock.

3. Mat a 4" x 6" photograph onto brown cardstock, then again onto blue cardstock.

4. Rubber-stamp the words "You Are" onto the bottom of the strip. Adhere or stitch strip to layout.

5. Mat a 5" x 7" photograph onto blue cardstock and adhere to layout at an angle.

6. Lightly adhere or tape twill to the bottom of the layout.

7. Machine stitch around photos using a straight stitch.

8. Zigzag stitch through the ribbon.

9. Finish the title using rub-on letters.

YOU ★ ARE

my ShiNing Star!

Ready or Not

Materials

Adhesive

Brads

Cardstock: mustard, navy blue, yellow

Computer and printer

Craft scissors

Ink

Mercerized cotton thread

Paper, patterned

Photographs

Sandpaper

Sewing machine

Instructions

1. Print journaling, birth stats, and photo captions onto pieces of mustard cardstock and trim to desired sizes.

2. Distress patterned paper by crumpling, sanding, and inking. Distress yellow cardstock by crumpling and sanding; however, make certain not to ink it. Tear to desired sizes.

3. Mat journaling block onto the distressed paper, then to yellow cardstock. Mat on 12"-square navy blue cardstock.

4. Stitch around top, right side, and bottom, following the edges of the ripped paper.

5. Wrapping one end of the birth stats strip around the back of the layout and slipping the other end beneath the journaling block, adhere to the bottom of the layout.

6. Straight stitch the journaling block along the edges of the torn patterned paper.

7. Adhere photographs where desired, and stitch around the edges.

8. Embellish page with brads and journal photo captions as desired.

On the day you were born — I was not convinced I was ready to be a Mother — I was also not convinced you were ready to be brought into this world.

Your original due date was September 16th — on the 21st Dr. Ewert told me I needed a Cesarean Section — you were late, weighed over 9 pounds & were breach. Since you were my first (and only) pregnancy they told that's the way it had to be. They did try to move you around (ouch!) but you were sitting cross legged and stubborn — you would not budge an inch in any direction. With strict orders to go to the emergency room if I thought I was in labor — I went home to get myself ready for my first ever stay in the hospital — *and* my first ever experience with having surgery. I was scared!

On Friday — the 24th — they performed a Cesarean Section at 10:00am to bring you into this world — I never felt a contraction - so I am not convinced that you were ready to face this big, bright, exciting world! I guess I was as prepared for motherhood as I could be — putting it off 1 or 2 more days would not have changed the fact that I was about to be a Mother - and it would *not* have changed who you turned out to be — I am wholly and totally thankful for that!

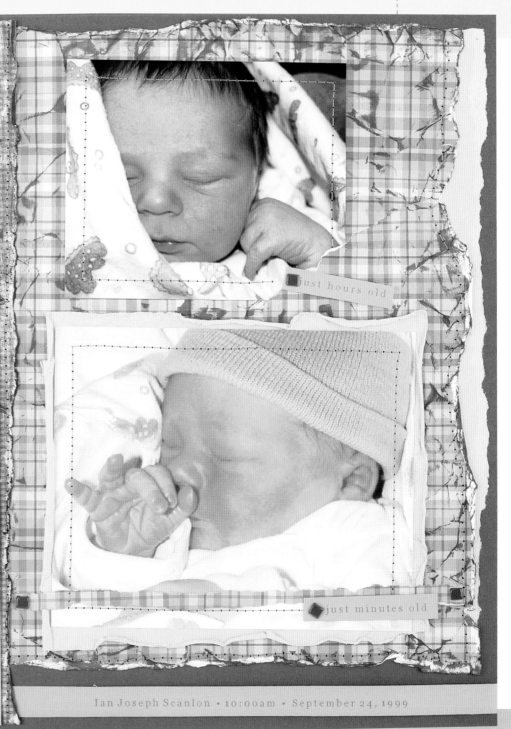

just hours old

just minutes old

Ian Joseph Scanlon • 10:00am • September 24, 1999

There's No Business Like Snow Business

Materials

- Acrylic paint
- Adhesive
- Cardstock, textured
- Chipboard letters
- Clear glaze
- Craft scissors
- Double-stick tape
- Foam stamps, alphabet
- Glitter paint, white
- Journaling tag
- Marker, pen, or desired journaling utensil
- Mercerized cotton thread
- Metal snowflake
- Monogram letter
- Paintbrush
- Ribbons: gingham and velvet
- Sewing machine (optional)
- Textured cardstock coin envelope
- Transparency
- Vellum, snowflake embossed

Instructions

1. Paint chipboard letters with glitter paint and allow to dry.

2. Spray with clear glaze and allow to dry.

3. Using acrylic paint, foam-stamp title onto transparency. Allow to dry.

4. Layer a strip of vellum onto white cardstock and attach a matted photograph using double-stick tape.

5. Adhere ribbon along the bottom edge of the layout, slightly overlapping the photograph.

6. Slide the bottom edges of the coin envelope and smaller photographs beneath ribbon. Stitch into place.

7. Stitch around the perimeter of all photographs and the edges of the layout.

8. Embellish page with chipboard letters, transparency title, and metal snowflake as desired.

9. Journal tag and slip into envelope.

theres no business LIKE SNOW business

Father & Son

I was so proud to see Sean with Conner during their visit to Maine. He's a young single father, juggling college, studying, and caring for a 3 year old on his own – WOW what an amazing guy. Conner is blessed to have such a great Dad.

father & son

Materials

- Acrylic paint
- Adhesive
- Bone folder
- Cardstock, textured
- Craft scissors
- Double-stick tape
- Marker
- Mercerized cotton thread
- Paintbrush
- Paper, patterned
- Pencil
- Ribbon
- Sewing machine with buttonhole foot or walking presser foot
- Transparency
- Twine

Instructions

1. On the backside of the patterned paper, pencil a border around the perimeter approximately ½" from the edge.

2. Using double-stick tape, place twine along the line. At each corner, make certain to cut the twine to ensure sharp edges.

3. Place double-stick tape over the twine and attach to a piece of cardstock.

4. Using bone folder, outline the twine under the patterned paper by running the blade lightly along either side of the twine. *Note: This will be helpful when sewing the page.*

5. Using a buttonhole foot or walking presser foot, sew as close to the twine as possible as shown in photograph, or as desired.

6. Using marker, print page title onto transparency. Paint the backside of the transparency with acrylic paint and allow to dry.

7. Stitch transparency title to page.

8. Embellish page with ribbon and any other desired materials.

Sticks

Materials

- Acrylic paint
- Adhesive
- Cardstock, textured
- Chipboard letters
- Colored twill
- Craft knife
- Craft scissors
- Denim letters
- Mercerized cotton thread
- Paper, desired colors
- Pencil
- Photographs
- Rub-on letters
- Sewing machine

Tip:

This project was inspired by the San Blas Appliqué technique used by the women in Panama. They create beautiful cloth works of art that incorporate brightly colored fabrics that are layered and stitched, then cut away to expose the layers beneath. Try researching this technique online for an array of inspiring patterns.

Instructions

1. Layer papers as desired and stitch together.

2. Pencil desired pattern onto a sheet of cardstock and machine stitch.

3. Using craft knife, cut away the portions that will expose other layers beneath.

4. To expose additional layers, place the cardstock over the layered papers and lightly pencil the spots that need to be cut away. Continue this process until desired look is achieved, as shown in photograph.

5. Machine stitch the top layer and photograph to layout.

6. Embellish by adhering or stitching chipboard, denim, and rub-on letters as desired.

I Need a Hero

Materials

Acrylic paint

Adhesive

Cardstock, textured

Computer and printer with word processing program

Craft scissors

Journaling tag

Marker, pen, or desired journaling utensil

Mercerized cotton thread

Metal letter

Paintbrush

Ribbon

Sewing machine

Transparency

Instructions

1. Create title in word processing program and print on transparency. *Note: I found that a transparency purchased at the office supply store was the most effective for this project.*

2. On the reverse side of the transparency, cover the area where the text appears with acrylic paint. *Note: This will help the text stand out a bit.*

3. Leaving the side and top of one photograph open for hidden journaling pocket, adhere photographs and title transparency to layout. Stitch into place, alternating between straight stitch and zigzag.

4. Complete title adhering or stitching metal letter as desired.

5. Journal desired wording onto tag and slip into place behind photograph as shown, or as desired.

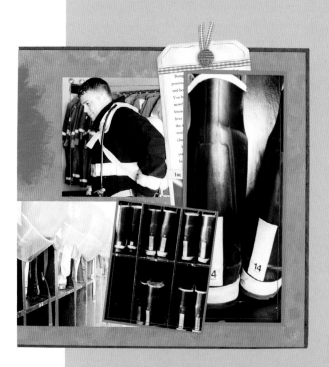

I need a hero

I'm holding out for a hero 'till the morning light. ......He's gotta be sure....and it's gotta be soon....He's gotta be larger than life.....I need a hero! Bonnie Tyler

Pink Sky at Night

Materials

Acrylic paint

Adhesive

Cardstock, textured

Clear stamps

Color washes

Craft scissors

Inkpads

Marker, pen, or desired journaling utensil

Mercerized cotton thread

Paper, patterned

Photographs

Preprinted journaling tag

Removable tape

Sewing machine

Shipping tags, extra large

Transparency

Twill

Zipper pulls

Instructions

1. Paint a square onto the backside of the transparency in a color suitable for a photo mat.

2. Adhere photographs where desired, then stitch them directly to the transparency.

3. Using removable tape, attach transparency to patterned paper, then stitch into place. Make certain to leave portions of the transparency unattached, in order to create pockets for the journaling tags. *Note: While stitching, make certain to not stitch over any pieces of removable tape. These pieces should be removed before stitching the area.*

4. Embellish oversized shipping tags by stamping, dyeing with color washes according to package directions, and journaling. Tie zipper pulls or twill to pre-punched holes, if desired. Insert tags into transparency pockets.

5. Adhere preprinted journaling tag as shown in photograph, or as desired.

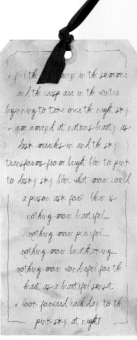

SUNSET

pink sky at night sailors

WISHE

FORM #072688 THERE'S A STUDY SOMEWHERE THAT SAYS
DREAMS THEY ARE, LIKE, 1000% MORE LIKELY TO COME

TO SEE
beauty
ev

3.
4.
5.
6.
7.
8.
9.
10.
what's the dream? what's the way? what's in the way?

DATE 2005   LOCATION Middletown

i feel the breeze in the summer
and the crisp air in the winter
beginning to take over the night sky.
i am amazed at nature, basically as
dusk marches in and the sky
transforms from a bright blue to pink

Chapter 6

Memorable Gifts, Tags & Cards

I find that handmade gifts, tags, and cards mean a little more because of the thought and effort that went into creating them. Stitching, whether by hand or machine, adds a particularly homey look, while also imparting unique texture and style. Make the next gift or card to a friend or family member especially memorable with the projects in this chapter.

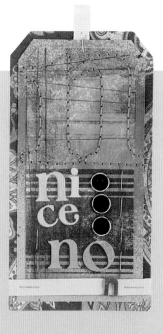
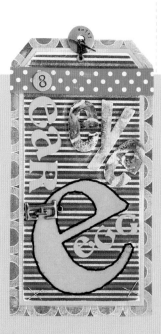

ABC Flash Cards & Box

Materials

- Acrylic paint
- Adhesive
- Alphabet charms
- Cardstock, textured
- Chalk
- Charms
- Color washes
- Crayon box
- Craft scissors
- Decoupage medium
- Letter stickers

- Mercerized cotton thread
- Metal letters
- Monogram-style die-cut letters
- Paintbrush
- Pencil
- Pen, platinum
- Rub-on letters
- Self-adhesive felt
- Sewing machine
- Twill
- Velvet ribbon
- Walnut ink and spray bottle

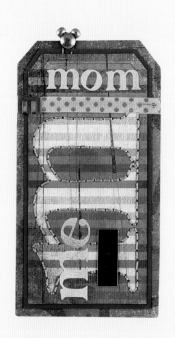

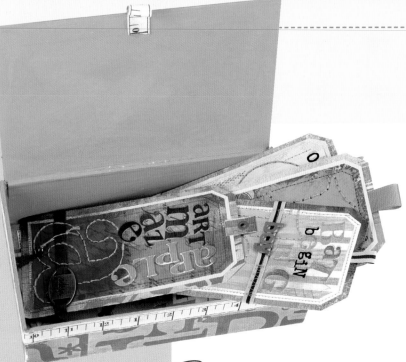

Flash Cards

1. Cut patterned paper into fifty-two 6¾" x 3¾" pieces. Cut coordinating cardstock into twenty-six 6¼" x 3¼" pieces. *Note: The patterned paper will be layered to either side of a piece of cardstock, so make certain to cut an even number of each paper in order to coordinate.*

2. Layer and adhere coordinating paper and cardstock to assemble twenty-six blank flash cards.

3. If desired, snip the top corners of each piece to resemble a tag, as shown in photograph.

4. Pencil the outline of each die-cut letter in various positions onto the cards.

5. Pierce holes along the outline of each letter.

6. Accentuate the areas that will be stitched using walnut ink, paint, chalk, color washes, or any other desired medium.

7. Straight stitch each letter. Machine stitch borders using various stitch types on each tag.

8. Embellish tags with ribbon, metal letters, and hand lettering as desired.

Box

9. Paint the inside of the crayon box and allow to dry.

10. Decoupage the outside of the box with coordinating patterned papers. Adhere felt to bottom for a finished look.

11. Adhere twill around the perimeter of the top edge of the box as shown.

12. Cut a small strip of twill and fold in half. Attach to box lid to function as a handle.

13. Trace "ABC" from the die-cut letters onto a sheet of patterned paper and paint around the letters.

14. Place the corresponding alphabet die-cuts over the "A" and "C" to act as temporary masks. Spray the entire sheet of paper with walnut ink two times, allowing to dry between applications. Remove the die-cuts when satisfied with the results.

15. Embellish with alphabet rub-ons.

16. Machine stitch a border around the letters for added interest.

17. Adhere decorated patterned paper to box lid.

Children's Book Photo Folio

Materials

Adhesive

Assorted ribbon

Beads

Brads, crystal

Cardstock, textured

Children's book

Colored flax

Craft scissors

Double-stick tape

Mercerized cotton thread

Paint chip sample

Paper, patterned

Photograph frame

Photographs

Ribbons

Ruler

Sewing machine

Silk flowers

Zipper pull

Instructions

1. Remove all pages or decorative papers from the book so that front cover, back cover, and thin spine are all that remain.

2. Lay the book out flat on your work surface, with the inside face down, and measure the length and width. Stitch patterned papers together along the edges to create a larger sheet of paper to fit the covers of the book. *Note: For additional support, I used both zigzag and straight stitches horizontally, then added a ribbon along the vertical seam using a variegated stitch pattern.*

3. Attach paper to book using double-stick tape. Make certain to fold the paper at the seam on each side of the spine to ensure proper closure.

4. Fold any excess paper to the inside of the folio and miter the corners.

5. Cut two 3" lengths of ribbon. Fold them both in half and adhere them to the front and back covers as shown in photograph.

6. Stitch around the edges of the folio using a variegated stitch.

7. To decorate the cover, cut a 6" length of ribbon and thread through the hole in the photograph frame. Match the ends together and, using a second piece of ribbon, tie a bow as close to the frame as possible.

8. Attach charm to frame using colored flax.

9. Use a brad to attach a flower and the frame to the folio as shown.

10. Embellish with additional flowers, if desired.

11. Adhere photographs and other desired ephemera to the front cover.

12. Cover the inside of the folio with coordinating papers and matted photos.

13. Embellish the spine with various coordinating ribbons, flowers, and beads by adhering, stitching, or attaching with brads, as desired.

Tip:

This is the perfect project for using old books your children have outgrown. You can also try combing yard sales or dollar stores to find material.

87

Gift-Size Photo Folio

Materials

Adhesive

Chipboard

Clear craft glue

Coin envelopes, white

Craft scissors

Decorative paper

Mercerized cotton thread

Metal accents

Metal clasp or frog

Mini-tag book

Pigment brush pad, scarlet

Photo corners: metal, paper

Printed fabric, yin yang pattern

Ribbon

Stickers

Instructions

1. Trim two pieces of chipboard to 5" x 7".

2. Cut fabric to 7" x 18".

3. Leaving 1" in between, center and adhere the two chipboard pieces on the fabric side-by-side using craft glue. Allow to dry.

4. Fold the excess fabric over onto the chipboard pieces, mitering the corners so that the fabric lies as flat as possible. Adhere fabric to chipboard with craft glue. Allow to dry.

5. Using brightly colored thread, crazy stitch the entire surface area of the fabric as shown in photograph. *Note: This will add detail along with helping to secure the fabric in any areas missed with glue.* Add ribbon, if desired.

6. Stitch metal clasp or frog components to the front and back covers of the folio as shown.

7. Embellish folio with metal photo corners.

8. Line the inside of the folio with decorative paper and embellish with stickers, ribbon, mini-tag book, coin envelopes for hidden journaling, or as desired.

9. Place paper photo corners on the inside of the folio so that the photograph can be easily changed or updated.

Friends Are the Flowers
We Pick for Ourselves

Materials

Acrylic paint

Adhesive

Brads

Cardstock, textured

Chipboard letters

Craft scissors

Foam stamps

Paper: fiber and patterned

Rub-on letters

Self-adhesive preprinted tabs

Stapler

Velvet ribbon

Instructions

1. Cut three approximately 4" x 7" tags from cardstock.

2. Cut three approximately 3¾" x 6¾" tags from coordinating cardstock, then center and adhere to tags cut in Step 1.

3. Embellish tags with stitching, chipboard letters, fiber paper, rub-on letters, brads, and tailored tabs.

4. Line up tags side by side as shown in photograph. Staple velvet ribbon along the seams to attach three tags together.

Tip:

Try making a custom envelope from cardstock and scrap patterned paper to tuck the card into before sending to a friend.

Dream Baby Brag Book

Materials

- Acrylic paint
- Adhesive
- Bone folder
- Cardstock
- Chipboard letters
- Craft scissors
- Eyelets (2)
- Eyelet setter
- Foam stamps
- Hook-and-loop tape
- Journaling tags
- Mercerized cotton thread
- Metal embellishment tags
- Paper: decorative, patterned
- Photographs
- Photo turns
- Ribbon
- Rub-on letters
- Scrapbooking pen
- Self-adhesive letter tags
- Sewing machine
- Thumbtack brads
- Twill

Instructions

1. Referring to photo, cut purse from cardstock.

2. Cut two 9" strips of patterned paper and lightly adhere to the outside of the purse as shown in photograph.

3. Machine stitch with coordinating thread, varying between straight and decorative stitches.

4. Score and fold purse in half.

5. Cut a 4" x 12" strip of cardstock. Score and fold in two spots to make a three-fold card. Double-mat on decorative paper and cardstock.

6. Adhere three-fold card inside of the purse as shown. Adhere photographs to the inside of the card, then decorate the outside with foam stamps and self-adhesive tags.

7. Repeat Step 5 to make a second three-fold card. Stitch the bottom of this card together so that the top remains open and creates a pocket.

8. Embellish with photo turns, self-adhesive tags, hidden journaling, or as desired.

9. Insert desired photos or journaling into the pocket.

10. Add eyelets to top of purse. Tie ribbon to create handle.

11. Embellish the outside of the purse with chipboard and rub-on letters. Add hook-and-loop tape and a photo turn to keep purse closed.

Cherished Baby Memories Card

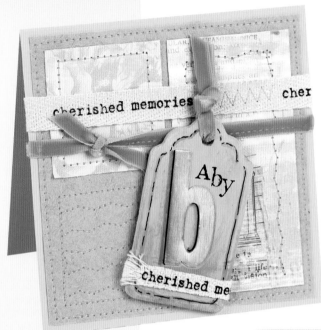

Materials

Acrylic paint

Adhesive

Cardstock: textured pink, textured pale yellow

Craft scissors

Envelope

Marker, platinum

Mercerized cotton thread

Metal "B"

Paintbrush

Paper, patterned

Rub-on letters

Sewing machine

Transparent envelope

Twill, printed

Velvet ribbon

Wooden tag

Instructions

1. Trim a small square and a small rectangle from patterned paper and adhere to a sheet of pink cardstock as shown in photograph.

2. Mat on yellow cardstock and stitch around the edges, varying between stitches.

3. In the blank area of the pink cardstock, stitch a square and fill in with various stitches.

4. Lightly adhere velvet ribbon and twill to layout, then secure by stitching into place.

5. Paint wooden tag and allow to dry.

6. Adhere metal "B" and twill to tag, then embellish as desired with rub-on letters. Attach to layout with a short length of ribbon.

7. Insert card into envelope.

CD Memory Case

Materials

Acrylic paint

Adhesive

Canvas

Cardboard CD case

Charm

Craft scissors

Envelope

Library pocket

Mercerized cotton thread

Monogram-style or paper letter

Needle

Paintbrush

Paper, patterned

Photographs

Ribbon slide

Ribbons, various

Ruler

Sandpaper

Sewing machine

Waxed thread

Instructions

1. Sand off the printed finish from all sides of the CD case. Apply a coat of acrylic paint to seal.

2. Measure the size of the CD case and trim patterned paper to fit, allowing a bit of acrylic paint to show on the top and bottom.

3. Stitch around the edges, varying between stitches.

4. Tear a piece of canvas to fit on the front cover as shown. Slowly stitch monogram or paper letter to canvas, then adhere canvas to CD case.

5. Embellish by stitching or adhering ribbon, charms, or other materials as desired.

6. To hold CD in place, wrap necessary length of 1½"-wide ribbon vertically around the inner flap. Stitch ribbon along the top and bottom edges. *Note: This will allow for two CDs to be stored in the case.*

7. Adhere library pocket to inside flap as shown. Insert journaling or CD contents into flap.

8. Adhere desired photographs to remaining folds.

9. Insert case into custom or purchased envelope to mail.

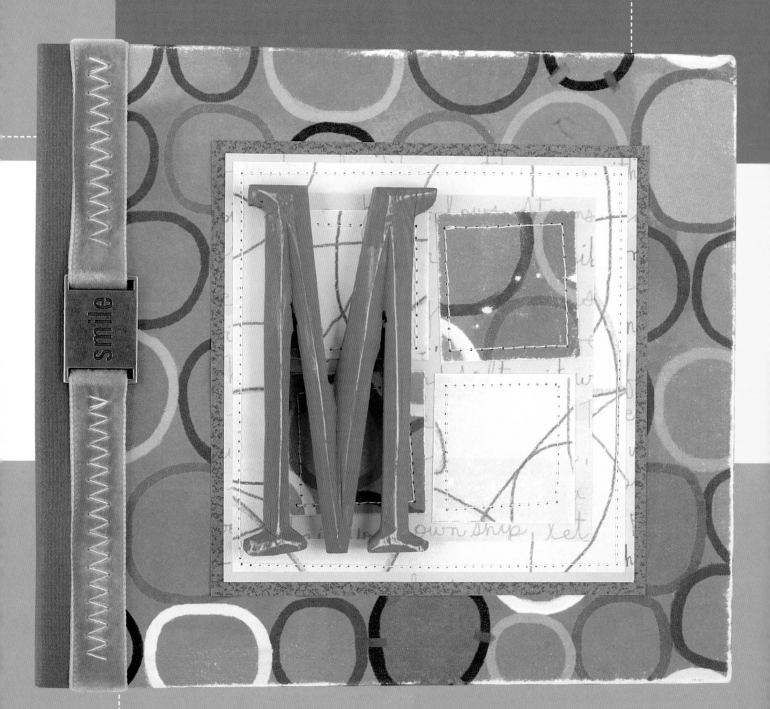

Chapter 7

Inspirational Mini-Books

Stitching has been used to secure book spines for centuries. The mini-book projects in this chapter put a spin on the ages-old technique with various types of bindings. Not only does stitching keep these books fastened, it also adds singular detail.

My Favorite Recipes from Mom

Materials

Acrylic paint

Adhesive

Cardstock, textured

Craft scissors

Decorative cocktail toothpicks

Eyelets

Eyelet setter

Foam stamps

Heavy-duty waxed thread

Journaling tags, large

Mercerized cotton thread

Needle

Paper, patterned

Paper punch, 1/16" diameter

Pencil

Photographs

Recipe cards with favorite recipes

Ribbon

Sewing machine

Silver charms

Instructions

1. Machine stitch various patterned papers and ribbons to the book cover to embellish. Slide toothpicks under the stitches to use as tabs for opening the recipe book.

2. Trim a piece of cardstock to 6" x 12". Trim patterned paper to fit, and adhere only the long edges to the cardstock.

3. Repeat Step 2 twice.

4. Fold each of these pages in half to 6" square. Mark four coordinating spots along the fold of each page, then punch holes.

5. Mark and punch coordinating holes in the cover. Insert eyelets to prevent the book from tearing.

6. Using waxed thread, bind each set of pocket pages to the cover separately, tying the knot on the outside of the book cover.

7. Embellish the spine by adhering or stitching ribbon and charms as desired.

8. Slip favorite recipes and journaling tags into the pockets. Add photographs of the people the recipes came from, if desired.

Tip:

To vary the types of pocket pages, try attaching 2"–3" strips of patterned paper to the bottom of the cardstock to create a half-pocket. Or, fold a 9" x 12" piece of cardstock up to create the pocket.

MOM

- Potato Soup
- Cocoa Brownies
- Zuchini Relish
- Steamed Lobster
- Cherry Winks

moose river · june 2005

The Joy of Life Paper Bag Book

Materials

Acrylic paint

Adhesive

Brown lunch bags (6)

Cardstock, textured

Chipboard letters

Craft scissors

Double-stick tape

Fabric

Foam stamps

Mercerized cotton thread

Paperclips

Ribbon

Sewing machine

Twine

Instructions

1. Trim the bottoms from five paper bags, so that 8½" remain.

2. Machine stitch or double-stick tape the side gussets of the individual bags together.

3. Align the top edges of all five bags together and secure with paperclips.

4. Fold the bottom edges over two times and secure with double-stick tape.

5. Slowly machine stitch the folded-over bottom edges in zigzag, making certain sewing machine can handle the thickness.

6. Trim the sixth paper bag to 8¾". Wrapping bag around stitched edge of stack, adhere into place to create a smooth, bound edge.

7. Stitch a 1½"-wide ribbon, fabric strip, or piece of patterned paper around the binding.

8. Embellish pages with paper, cardstock, photographs, or various found objects as desired.

9. Slip journaled tags, photographs, or any other memorabilia into the pockets.

Sometimes your joy
is the source of your
smile – but
sometimes your smile
can be the source of
your joy.

Thich Nhat Hanh

Each friend represents a
world in us, a world not
born until they
arrive, and it is only by
this meeting that a new
world is born.

Anais Nin

A thing of
beauty is a joy
forever.

John Keats

I Love You Paper Bag Card

Materials

Adhesive

Brown lunch bags (2)

Cardstock, red textured

Charms

Craft scissors

Decorative-edged scissors

Fabric glue

Felt, red

Marker, pen, or desired journaling utensil

Mercerized cotton thread

Metal letters

Needle

Note card

Paper flowers

Paper, patterned

Pencil

Photograph

Ribbon

White eraser

Instructions

1. Referring to Steps 1–5 of The Joy of Life Paper Bag Book on pages 98–99, trim the bottoms from paper bags.

2. Cover the front and back of the paper bag booklet with patterned paper.

3. Cut a strip of red cardstock and scallop the edges with decorative-edged scissors. Adhere to the binding and stitch into place.

4. Adhere felt to paper bag booklet with fabric glue as shown in photograph. Allow to dry.

5. Stitch ribbon onto felt as shown.

6. Lightly pencil random hearts onto felt and slowly stitch them using thread of contrasting color. Erase any remaining pencil lines.

7. Embellish the spine by adhering or stitching paper flowers, metal letters, and charms, as desired.

8. Stitch a similar heart pattern to a second piece of felt and adhere inside the card.

9. Add a photograph and journal a private note to tuck inside.

I LOVE YOU

Materials

- Adhesive
- Canvas
- Cardstock, textured
- Corrugated cardboard
- Craft scissors
- Decoupage medium
- Denim snaps
- Drill and drill bits (optional)
- Fabric dye
- Fabric glue
- Fabric, paper, or metal letter
- Heavy-duty craft glue
- Hole punch, ¾" diameter
- Mercerized cotton thread
- Metal album corners
- Needle
- Page protector or album page
- Paper, patterned
- Pencil
- Ring binder
- Walnut ink and spray bottle

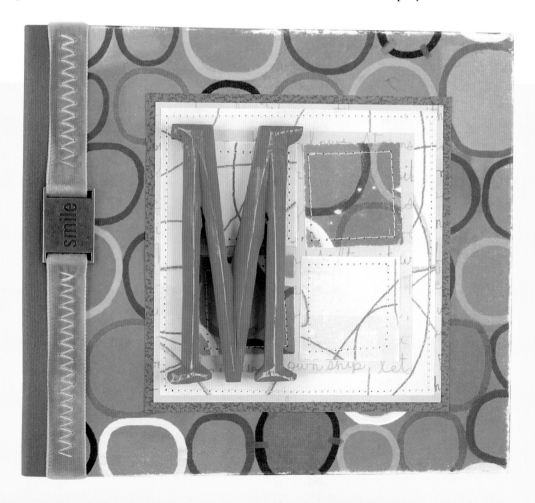

Instructions

1. Remove the metal spine and rings from the binder. *Note: It may be necessary to use a drill and drill bits for this part of the process.*

2. Cut cardboard into two equal pieces for the front and back covers. Cut a third piece for the spine, making certain it is wide enough to accommodate the ring binder.

3. Trim a piece of canvas so that it measures 1" larger than the spine on all sides. Following package directions, dye the canvas to match patterned paper. Spray with walnut ink and crumple while wet. Allow to dry.

4. Use a heavy coat of decoupage medium to adhere patterned paper to the outside of the front and back covers. Allow to dry, setting heavy object on top so piece dries flat. *Note: Any bubbles that may appear will generally disappear once the piece has dried; however, make certain to manipulate the paper to avoid bulges and gaps.*

5. Apply fabric glue to the cardboard spine and center on canvas. Allow to dry.

6. Stitch around the perimeter of the spine to create a border. Fill in the border with crazy stitching. Make certain not to turn the edges of the canvas over to the inside of the album.

7. If desired, cover additional cardboard pieces with canvas and stitch to covers to create pockets. Additional stitching may also be added to embellish.

8. Apply craft glue to the excess canvas on either side of the spine. Place the covers face down on the canvas, leaving a very small gap of approximately $\frac{1}{16}$" between the spine and each cover. Place a heavy object over the cardboard pieces and allow to dry completely.

9. Fold the excess canvas that hangs over the top and bottom to the inside of the album and glue down. Allow to dry completely.

10. Stitch around the outside edges of the album to secure the spine and covers together, as well as to create a nice border.

11. Line the inside of the front and back covers with patterned paper or cardstock, making certain the seam of the papers meet in the spot where the binder rings will be placed. Place something heavy onto the cardboard pieces and allow to dry completely.

12. To ensure correct placement, place a page protector or album page onto the binder rings. Adjust the binder rings until correct placement has been achieved. Mark the spots where the denim snaps will be placed and punch them out using a $\frac{3}{4}$" hole punch.

13. Attach denim snaps according to manufacturer's instructions.

14. Attach metal album corners to each corner to complete the album.

15. Embellish front cover with fabric, paper, or metal letter that corresponds with baby's name, as desired.

pinch me

Am I going to wake up from this
fantastic dream called my life?

I can hardly believe I am where I
am – and only 39 years old!
Married to the man of my
dreams, living in Rhode Island,
and designing all day long. Ian
goes to private school, I
volunteer in the classroom most
every week getting involved in
what he does every day. Inviting
him to get involved in what I do
everyday. Gotta LOVE IT. I
work one day a week – at a job I
absolutely love – for a woman
who is an amazing cancer
survivor. What more could a
person want from life?
I am in a good spot. It's taken a
while to get here – all I can say is

it 's a wonderful life...

Chapter 8

Quilt Blocks

I have always loved the look of quilt blocks and appliqués, so I saw no reason why I couldn't adapt the technique using my favorite medium, paper. Piecing together various patterns of paper and stitching them to a page will achieve that cozy, quilted look for your scrapbook pages and other paper projects.

Mother

Materials

Adhesive

Cardstock, textured

Clear stamps

Craft scissors

Eyelets

Eyelet setter

Flower brads

Inkpads

Mercerized cotton thread

Paper, patterned and plain

Paper punch, flower

Pre-printed alphabet cards

Rubber stamps

Sewing machine

Twill

Instructions

1. Mount patterned paper onto cardstock.

2. Lightly adhere alphabet cards to patterned paper, leaving spaces in between as shown in photograph. *Note: My alphabet cards spell out "MOTHER"; however, this page can be customized for anyone you wish.*

3. Trim scrap paper to fit the spaces between the cards and adhere to the page.

4. Punch flowers from plain paper.

5. Adhere photograph and flower punches as desired.

6. Zigzag stitch around the alphabet cards and patterned paper to machine appliqué them to the page.

7. Embellish as desired with twill, eyelets, and rubber-stamping.

Tip:

If you love the look of quilted blocks on your page, but don't want to take the time to cut them to the correct size, simply use preprinted embellishments or cards as the blocks. Zigzag stitch them down and fill in empty spaces with various pieces of scrap paper. If the seams don't look right, hide them with a paper punch or two.

MOTHER

M O T H
E
R

Mom
a treasure
happy ✱✱
● is sweet
love you ●
silly ● joy
fun!
believe in
✱me✱
my friend

Guinness Stout: The Coach Dog

Materials

Acrylic paint

Adhesive

Cardstock: black and red textured

Craft scissors

Dog tag

Double-stick tape

Foam stamps, alphabet

Marker, grey

Mercerized cotton thread

Metal ruler

Papers: paw print and other patterned

Photocopier

Razor blade

Sewing machine

Shipping tags

Instructions

1. Choose a quilt block pattern from the fabric store or online and make a photocopy, enlarging or reducing as desired.

2. Layer papers that will be used for quilt block together using removable double-stick tape.

3. Attach quilt block photocopy to the top of all layered paper with removable double-stick tape.

4. Using a metal ruler and razorblade, cut quilt block components out. *Note: This process will allow you to create two quilt blocks exactly opposite each other by cutting the same components from all the layered papers.*

5. As each component is cut, adhere it to the coordinating spot on the cardstock base.

6. Trim quilt block to desired size and mat on coordinating cardstock.

7. Machine stitch around block.

8. Add any desired embellishments.

9. Adhere block to page, leaving the top open for journaled shipping tags.

10. Foam stamp title in acrylic paint and allow to dry.

11. Shadow title with grey marker.

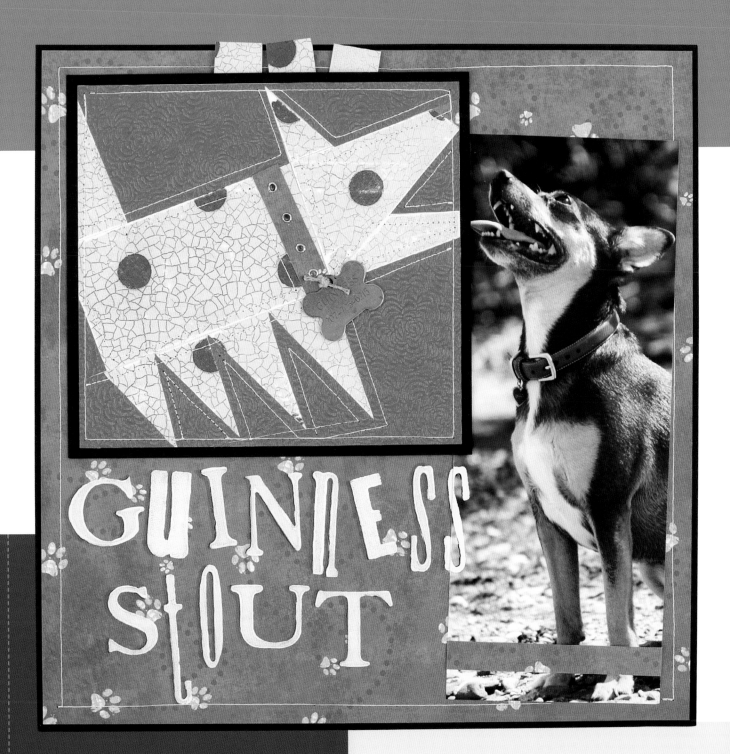

GUINNESS STOUT

Pinch Me

Materials

Acrylic paint

Adhesive

Aerosol paper preserving spray

Canvas

Cardstock, textured

Computer and printer

Craft scissors

Fabric paper

Mercerized cotton thread

Paintbrush

Paper, patterned

Photo frames

Photograph

Photo mat

Sewing machine

Stapler

Transparency

Twill

Instructions

1. Print photograph on canvas, referring to printer user's manual.

2. Spray with aerosol paper preserving spray and set aside to dry.

3. Cut four 2¾" squares from patterned paper or fabric paper and trim from corner to corner to make eight triangles.

4. Trim photograph to desired size and double-mat on patterned paper and cardstock.

5. Arrange triangles in desired position, adhere to page, then hand stitch around the edge of each triangle.

6. Print title and journaling onto transparency. Dry brush acrylic paint onto back of transparency to enhance readability of the journaling.

7. Slide transparency under photo mat and lightly adhere.

8. Cut pieces of coordinating paper, twill, and fabric paper. Varying between each of these materials, create a random border around the page, stitching or stapling into place.

9. Cut photo corners from fabric paper. While stitching around the edge of the photograph, stitch photo corners into place.

10. Embellish page by adhering or stitching twill and photo frames to layout as desired.

pinch me

Am I going to wake up from this fantastic dream called my life?

I can hardly believe I am where I am – and only 39 years old! Married to the man of my dreams, living in Rhode Island, and designing all day long. Ian goes to private school, I volunteer in the classroom most every week getting involved in what he does every day. Inviting him to get involved in what I do everyday. Gotta LOVE IT. I work one day a week – at a job I absolutely love – for a woman who is an amazing cancer survivor. What more could a person want from life? I am in a good spot. It's taken a while to get here – all I can say is

it 's a wonderful life...

Every friend is to the other a sun and a sunflower too.

Anita's Garden

August · 2005

Chapter 9

Paper, Fabric & Stitching

Mixing mediums is an interesting way to approach projects. Depending on the materials, the combination will be a dynamic contrast or a pleasing complement. Fabric and paper are the latter. They are easily combined because you can stitch them together, and fabric adds such an appealing, soft texture to paper projects.

There's Something in Your Eyes

Materials

Adhesive

Cardstock, textured

Charms

Craft scissors

Fabric, patterned

Inkpad

Marker, pen, or desired journaling utensil

Paper, patterned

Photo corners

Photograph

Platinum marker

Rubber stamps

Sewing machine

Silver beads

Stickers

Tags

Twine

Waxed thread

Instructions

1. Adhere photograph to cardstock, then stitch photo into place, including photo corners.

2. Mat on patterned paper, then onto patterned fabric. Crazy stitch to layout, leaving one side open for hidden journaling.

3. Handprint various words defining the photograph's subject onto coordinating cardstock. Trim close to the text. Beginning in the center of each word block, stitch into place, then stitch a border around the perimeter.

4. Stamp title onto layout, then create a shadow with platinum marker. Finish title by stamping last word directly onto photograph.

5. Handprint journaling onto cardstock.

6. Embellish page by tying, adhering, or stitching twine, charms, tags, and stickers as desired.

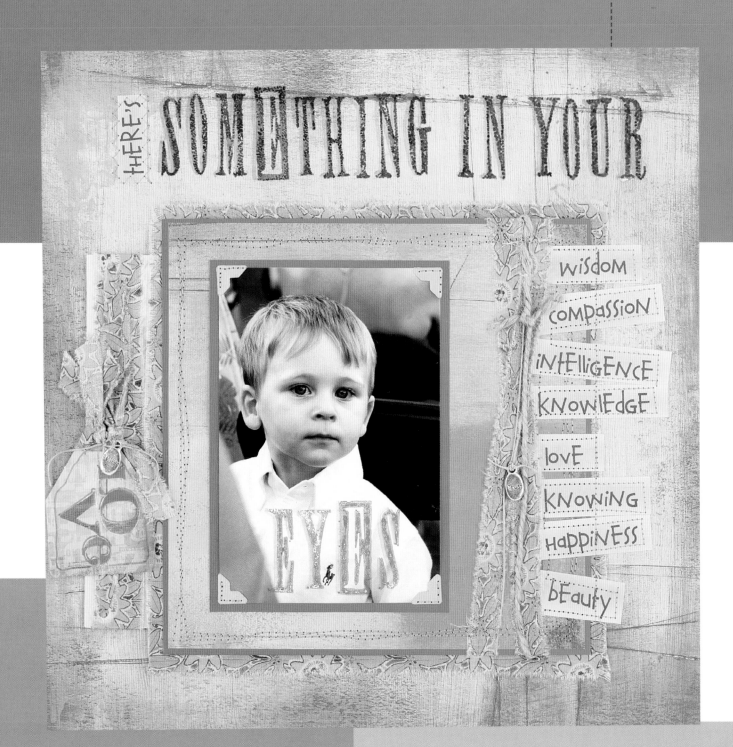

tHERE'S **SOMETHING IN YOUR**

EYES

WiSdOM
COMPaSSioN
iNtElliGENCE
KNoWlEdGE
loVE
KNOWiNG
HaPPiNESS
bEauty

Time Will Tell

Materials

Adhesive

Cardstock, textured

Computer with photo-editing program and printer

Craft scissors

Embossing ink

Fabric, yin yang pattern

Fortune cookies

Grosgrain ribbon

License plate-style metal embellishment

Marker, pen, or desired journaling utensil

Mercerized cotton thread

Paper, patterned

Red chalk

Rubber stamps

Sandpaper

Sewing machine

Instructions

1. Tear a strip of the fabric and crazy quilt to cardstock using brightly colored thread.

2. Stitch a length of ribbon along the edge of the fabric and adhere to layout as shown in photograph.

3. Using a photo-editing program, add title to the photograph. Print in black-and-white and allow to dry. Coat with photo preserving spray.

4. Sand the edges of the photo to distress, and stitch to layout as shown.

5. Stamp a sheet of white paper with embossing ink, then rub chalk over the stamped images to create custom patterned paper.

6. Handprint journaling on custom patterned paper and trim to size.

7. Crack fortune cookies open and remove fortunes. Stitch or adhere fortunes to the layout.

TIME

will tell

where I'll be in a year! For me to predict where I'll be - I must look at where I have been. A designer at heart and by trade. I hope to live my dream to be a "preferred" designer for manufacturers showcasing new and inventive ways to use their products. An artist from the very beginning, I see myself following my heart and continuing to capture my dream. With a strong sense of home and family, I see the beginnings of a new home on our property in Maine near my family. Planning, designing, breaking ground and moving on to the next chapter in our lives is a dream I see coming to fruition. So many things in the works - but only time will tell where I'll be in a year. My hope, my family and my heart will guide me there!

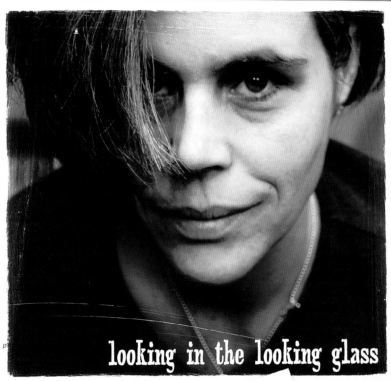

looking in the looking glass

A smile is your personal welcome mat.

Handsome is that does.

Your virtues are your priceless treasures.

From now on your kindness will lead you to success.

Your winsome smile sure protection.

Nothing in the world is accomplished without passion.
Lucky Numbers 4, 8, 15, 3°

Prejudice is the child of ignorance.

Good food brings good health and longevity.
Lucky Numbers 4, 8, 10, 13, 41.

Wish you happiness.

Have a beautiful day.

Your talents will be recognized and suitably rewarded.
Lucky Numbers 17, 20, 24, 25, 32, 38

You are busy but you are happy.

You will take a chance in something in near future.

Smile to others, honesty and friendship bring you fortune.
Lucky Numbers 12, 14, 16, 24, 26, 28

Autumn

Materials

Adhesive

Cardstock, black textured

Computer and printer

Decorative fibers

Inkpads

Iron and ironing board

Iron-on transfer sheet

Mercerized cotton thread

Muslin

Paper, patterned

Photographs

Rubber stamps

Sewing machine

Silk leaves

Walnut ink and spray bottle

Instructions

1. Print an 8½" x 11" photograph onto iron-on transfer sheet according to printer user's manual.

2. Spritz muslin with walnut ink and allow to dry. Tear edges to create a tattered look.

3. Iron photograph from transfer sheet onto muslin.

4. Mat muslin onto patterned paper, then onto cardstock.

5. Stamp title onto a strip of cardstock. Adhere title and silk leaves to page as shown in photograph.

6. Stitch around title and along the spine of the leaves.

7. To create matching page, mat three photographs onto one sheet of cardstock, as shown, and stitch around the perimeters.

8. Mat one small photograph to cardstock and adhere in the center of the three larger photographs. Stitch around the edges of the small photo.

9. Adhere silk leaves along the bottom of the page, and stitch along the spines.

10. Trim cardstock to desired size. Fold in half and stitch desired edges together, leaving the top or one side open to create a pocket. Embellish by adhering or stitching a leaf, paper scraps, or decorative fibers to pocket, or as desired.

11. Stitch decorated pocket to layout.

U Pick Lavender

Materials

Acrylic paint

Adhesive

Aerosol paper preserving spray

Canvas

Cardstock, textured

Chipboard letters

Computer and inkjet printer

Double-tipped shading marker

Fine-point black marker

Mercerized cotton thread

Mesh fabric

Paper, patterned

Photographs

Rub-on letters

Sewing machine

Instructions

1. Print photograph on canvas that has been prepped for use with an inkjet printer, referring to printer user's manual. Allow to dry.

2. Spray canvas with aerosol paper preserving spray and allow to dry.

3. Hand-color photograph with double-tipped marker, coloring and shading as necessary. Outline the edges of the image in select places with black marker.

4. Mat canvas onto cardstock, then again onto patterned paper or fabric.

5. Machine stitch around the edges of the patterned paper using the blind hemstitch function. *Note: Set machine to a stitch length of 2 and stitch width of 6 for this border.* Make certain to leave plenty of space for journaling around the photograph.

6. Layer mesh fabrics and photographs at the bottom of the layout and hand stitch using cotton thread.

7. Add one small photograph and machine stitch a straight border around the edges.

8. Paint some of the chipboard letters and cover others in paper, as desired, to create title. Adhere to page.

9. Complete the layout with rub-on letters.

U
PICK
{SEQUIM}
LAVENDER

the lavender at Purple Haze Lavender farm was the most beautiful color. to close my eyes and smell their relaxing scent made me feel like I was in heaven.

U Pick

Beauty

Materials

Adhesive

Cardstock, textured

Craft scissors

Flower template

Iron and ironing board

Mercerized cotton thread

Paintbrush

Paper, patterned

Paper punch

Rub-on letters

Wool thread

Instructions

1. Wet a piece of cardstock and crumple. *Note: This will create texture for the completed flower.* Hot iron to dry and flatten.

2. Using a flower template, cut out various sizes of flowers from the crumpled cardstock. Punch out the centers.

3. Mat a photograph onto cardstock. Mat onto patterned paper and cardstock base.

4. Varying between stitches, stitch flowers to layout using various colors of thread and yarn. Dry brush the edges of flowers with acrylic paint as desired.

5. Complete layout by adding title using rub-on letters.

Tip:

This technique is wonderful for emulating silk flowers when you cannot find ones to match your layout.

Anita's Garden

Materials

- Acrylic paint
- Adhesive
- Bead
- Cardstock, textured
- Chipboard sunflower
- Marker, pen, or desired writing utensil
- Needle
- Paper, patterned
- Pencil
- Photographs
- Sewing machine
- Silk flower (optional)
- Stapler (optional)
- Wool thread
- Yarn

Instructions

1. Mount cardstock and lightly mark shapes and lines to be stitched.

2. Pierce the shapes with a needle and hand stitch with various colors of yarn.

3. Varying the width of the zigzag, machine stitch the remainder of the paper.

4. Complete layout by adding preprinted patterned paper, photographs, and desired embellishments, such as silk flower and journaled caption stapled to page.

About the Author

Catherine Matthews-Scanlon was raised in rural Maine, where she has lived for the majority of her life. She is the only daughter and youngest of three siblings, and tries to spend as much time with her family as possible. Catherine currently resides in Rhode Island with her husband, Joe, and their son, Ian, who is seven. They have traveled extensively throughout the U.S., as her husband serves in the military.

Catherine holds a degree in printing and graphic design and currently teaches scrapbooking and altered art classes. She spends her days at work in her studio, enjoying the company of her rat terrier, Guinness, who is just as much a part of the family as anyone.

Acknowledgments

There are so many people to thank—those who have touched my life in a major way and those who have inspired and encouraged me to do my best. Some are nameless as I have chatted here and there with so many people. Thank you to all that remain nameless in my head but vivid in my imagination! A *huge* thanks to my loving and supportive husband, who cleaned, cooked, and grocery shopped while I was locked in my studio creating. To my little man Ian who was so understanding when I had to work, and who *loves* everything I make. Thanks guys, you rock.

A big standing applause to Cindy Weloth for discovering me and to Ana Maria Ventura for her endless hours of editing and support. Thank you to all those at Chapelle who have worked so hard to make this book so beautiful to look at. Thanks to Vicki, Libby, and Gretchen for your wonderful contributions. You guys are awesome. Thanks to Joanie for your wonderful encouragement and input. You got me through this with your constant support. THANKS to everyone.

Last, but not least, a huge heartfelt thanks to my parents for believing in me and for molding me into the person that I am today. Without your help, support, love, and inspiration, I wouldn't be where I am. Thank you to Tammy, Jeff, and Sean for letting me photograph your kids, and for having beautiful kids to photograph!

Note about Suppliers

Usually, the supplies you need for making the projects in Lark books can be found at your local craft supply store, discount mart, home improvement center, or retail shop relevant to the topic of the book. Occasionally, however, you may need to buy materials or tools from specialty suppliers. In order to provide you with the most up-to-date information, we have created a list of suppliers on our Web site, which we update on a regular basis. Visit us at www.larkbooks.com, click on "Craft Supply Sources," and then click on the relevant topic. You will find numerous companies listed with their web address and/or mailing address and phone number.

Metric Equivalency Chart

inches to millimeters and centimeters						
inches	mm	cm	inches	cm	inches	cm
⅛	3	0.3	9	22.9	30	76.2
¼	6	0.6	10	25.4	31	78.7
½	13	1.3	12	30.5	33	83.8
⅝	16	1.6	13	33.0	34	86.4
¾	19	1.9	14	35.6	35	88.9
⅞	22	2.2	15	38.1	36	91.4
1	25	2.5	16	40.6	37	94.0
1¼	32	3.2	17	43.2	38	96.5
1½	38	3.8	18	45.7	39	99.1
1¾	44	4.4	19	48.3	40	101.6
2	51	5.1	20	50.8	41	104.1
2½	64	6.4	21	53.3	42	106.7
3	76	7.6	22	55.9	43	109.2
3½	89	8.9	23	58.4	44	111.8
4	102	10.2	24	61.0	45	114.3
4½	114	11.4	25	63.5	46	116.8
5	127	12.7	26	66.0	47	119.4
6	152	15.2	27	68.6	48	121.9
7	178	17.8	28	71.1	49	124.5
8	203	20.3	29	73.7	50	127.0

yards to meters									
yards	meters	yards	meters	yards	meters	yards	meters	yards	meters
⅛	0.11	2⅛	1.94	4⅛	3.77	6⅛	5.60	8⅛	7.43
⅛	0.11	2⅛	1.94	4⅛	3.77	6⅛	5.60	8⅛	7.43
¼	0.23	2¼	2.06	4¼	3.89	6¼	5.72	8¼	7.54
⅜	0.34	2⅜	2.17	4⅜	4.00	6⅜	5.83	8⅜	7.66
⅝	0.46	2½	2.29	4½	4.11	6½	5.94	8½	7.77
⅝	0.57	2⅝	2.40	4⅝	4.23	6⅝	6.06	8⅝	7.89
¾	0.69	2¾	2.51	4¾	4.34	6¾	6.17	8¾	8.00
⅞	0.80	2⅞	2.63	4⅞	4.46	6⅞	6.29	8⅞	8.12
1	0.91	3	2.74	5	4.57	7	6.40	9	8.23
1¼	1.03	3¼	2.86	5⅛	4.69	7¼	6.52	9⅛	8.34
1¼	1.14	3¼	2.97	5¼	4.80	7¼	6.63	9¼	8.46
1⅜	1.26	3⅜	3.09	5⅜	4.91	7⅜	6.74	9⅜	8.57
1½	1.37	3½	3.20	5½	5.03	7½	6.86	9½	8.69
1⅝	1.49	3⅝	3.31	5⅝	5.14	7⅝	6.97	9⅝	8.80
1¾	1.60	3¾	3.43	5¾	5.26	7¾	7.09	9¾	8.92
1⅞	1.71	3⅞	3.54	5⅞	5.37	7⅞	7.20	9⅞	9.03
2	1.83	4	3.66	6	5.49	8	7.32	10	9.14

Index

or ♥ silly ♥ friends ♥ love ♥ family ♥

like mother like daughter

mother and daughter

c & v

Count Your Blessings

MOM AND ME